SUPPLEMENTAL YET ESSENTIAL

Practical Training for Elder, Assisted Living, and Long-Term Care

JUDY SALISBURY

Supplemental Yet Essential: Practical Training for Elder, Assisted Living, and Long-Term Care
By Judy Salisbury

Published by Logos Presentations
1087 Lewis River Road, Suite #249
Woodland, WA 98674

The websites cited are for reference purposes only. Neither Judy Salisbury nor Logos Presentation intends the citing of any website, person, or organization as an endorsement unless specified.

Cover design created by Logos Presentations through *Canva*.

Printed in the United States of America.

Library of Congress Control Number: 2023915513
ISBN: 978-0-9657678-3-5

Kindle ISBN: 978-0-9657678-4-2
Hardback ISBN: 978-0-9657678-5-9

DEDICATED TO:

My incredible daughter-in-law,

Marie:

Your gracious and meticulous review, timely and appropriate suggestions, and encouragement were invaluable and so greatly appreciated for the success of this work that is so close to my heart. I know your input came with not only experience in Assisted Living and long-term nursing care in the mid-western and western United States but also a love that matches mine for those who need assistance, loving care, patience, and compassion.

May this work be useful for all those who share our love, concern, passion, and diligence to meet the needs of individuals who rely on loved ones or nursing for the quality medical, emotional, and spiritual care they so deserve. Thank you so much, *Precious*. Never stop lighting up every room!

With great love, affection, and gratitude,

Mom

TABLE OF CONTENTS

SECTION ONE

Avoid Revolving-Door Whiplash: A Fresh Approach To Retention And Success

1. A Fresh Perspective

Before I begin, thank you for your interest and desire to become better equipped as a leader in what I believe is one of the most unique settings for anyone to work. What makes it so special is that a career in long-term care or Assisted Living means working where other people live while being responsible for their medical care. Those of us who work, or have worked, in long-term care, hospice, rehabilitation, or Assisted Living know what I am talking about, and that is why this supplemental training, with immediate and practical application, is unique, timely, and essential.

The information in this book comes from decades of combined experience in leadership and training for various areas, including nursing, emergency medical services, emotional trauma care, and senior care. It is training that, when imparted to the appropriate members of Assisted Living, Elder, and long-term care staff, can boost morale, limit liability, and help save lives.

In these first few chapters, I hope to help you avoid the whiplash that managers, business owners, administrators, and directors can experience with the reoccurring turnover of staff that plagues many Care Centers. This turnover often critically overwhelms nursing staff. My goal is that the information supplied will help build confidence in your staff members as it also helps to sharpen or enhance their skills. What naturally follows as you implement this training is the recognition that you have invested in helping your staff to become better trained, more confident in their position, and content with their work environment leading to longevity and an increase in quality care, which is always the goal.

I will also address unique situations, like the relationship between staff, EMS, and 911 dispatchers. I will discuss appropriate ways to approach the Power of Attorney (POA) or family members for residents suffering from a medical emergency or traumatic injury that will help to alleviate tensions that can arise. As an individual with tactical training, I will also include life-saving thoughts if the unthinkable should happen at your Care Center. With that, let's get into our training!

EVOLVING ROLES AND MINDSETS

I think it is essential to acknowledge how roles have changed within nursing, and I believe an excellent article by Dr. Jordan Grumet expresses what many of us in healthcare think. It is appropriately entitled, *Doctors and Nurses are being Overloaded with Menial Tasks*:

> I'm no economist. In fact, I have never taken any business or accounting classes in my life. But it doesn't take a formal education to get this. We are speeding down the wrong path.
>
> The call at three in the morning woke me from a deep sleep. I fumbled and strained to hear the whispered voice of the apologetic nurse. Apparently Mrs. Thompson had scraped her arm against the wheelchair, and suffered a minor abrasion. No harm, no foul. Except that ever since the state had come in and eviscerated the nursing home protocols, extra precautions were being taken. Some things just won't be left till the morning anymore.
>
> My early trip to the hospital was no better. My personal assistant called to say that I had to redo the form to get one of my patients a

walker. Although I had signed it by hand, we had typed in the date. Apparently the medical equipment company required that the date also be written in ink. It sounds minor, but I had to find a fax machine, wait for the fax to arrive, write in the date, and fax back. All, of course, needed to be done immediately.

Luckily my hospitalized patient was getting better. And since it was neither an admission nor discharge day, I just might escape without wasting too much time on paperwork. As I was putting on my coat, the head nurse stopped me in my tracks.

"I just need to notify you that your patient claims she is missing fifty dollars, and can you sign this form acknowledging that you have been informed."

What? Since when did I become a policeman? Since when did I take charge of all criminal activities that take place inside the hospital walls?

Health care is being overrun. Government induced regulation and documentation are creating mental gridlock. The dictates of our forms and procedures are tying up those with the physical and intellectual know how to care for patients.

Why can't you get an appointment with your doctor? Why are diagnoses being missed? Why is the quality of health care in the United States declining rapidly? Stop querying big data and start looking at the hunched backs and sore

> shoulders of the people who are inputting that data.
>
> We are turning our physicians and nurses into scribes, field workers, and secretaries. Those who create the most value, who took the most time and money to train, are being overloaded with menial and level inappropriate tasks.
>
> No small business would be naive enough to operate this way. Why then, should one of the largest sectors of our economy?[1]

As you read that article, did you find yourself nodding in agreement regarding those hunched backs? When I came into nursing, I noticed that when Certified Nursing Assistants (CNAs) were trained as Medication Assistants (Med Aids), they helped to free up the Licensed Practical Nurses (LPNs). The LPNs could then turn to more hands-on patient care. However, as the article stated, I noticed that Registered Nurses (RNs) were more like administrators with hunchbacks in the nurse's station or hidden away in an office. Sadly, as the article states, those who invested so much time, education, and money have become disgruntled paper pushers.

There isn't much that can be done about the paper pushing. However, for RNs who recognize and are frustrated with the changes in nursing, whenever possible, they should get back to some hands-on patient care. If practical and consistent with protocol, it might be a good idea to actively maintain skills by being involved with hands-on patient care whenever possible. This hands-on approach helps keep them

---

https://www.kevinmd.com/2014/04/doctors-nurses-overloaded-menial-tasks.html For speaking inquiries please visit: jordangrumet.com

in touch with those they serve and gives them a clear understanding of those they lead while setting, as mentors, an example for their nursing staff to follow.

VARIED AND UNUSUAL PERSPECTIVE

I received my introduction to nursing at a pivotal time for the Care Center where I worked. At first, I felt like quite the outsider. However, observing through various lenses of my life experience, particular challenges were brought into focus, which enabled me to create solutions. A varied background will do that for anyone! To help you understand why I could recognize what others might have missed, perhaps I should share more of what I brought to the table when I stepped onto the floor as a caregiver in 2011.

My resume-building began in the 1980s when I worked in corporate sales and high-level customer service. I was an award-winning salesperson, then found myself in management, and eventually enjoyed training salespeople. By 1994 I founded an organization to train and equip individuals and groups across the United States with effective communication and presentation skills. The work has since expanded from there.

By 2005, I joined my husband as a volunteer firefighter in our local fire department. That same year I became an EMT with the department and eventually became an IV Tech. By 2010 I was certified as an EMS Evaluator/Instructor and a certified lay counselor, which I found very helpful when tasked to become my fire department's volunteer Crisis Care Counselor in 2017. Added to this varied and unusual background was that I had been the Power of Attorney (POA) for a loved one in a long-term care facility for a decade.

In 2011, I decided to attain a CNA license. The reason for this I will explain in a later chapter. I was immediately hired at my nearest Care Center and worked in hospice, long-term care, and rehabilitation. What I did not know when the Director of Nursing (DON) hired me was that the leadership had recently decided to have Med Aids pass medications to free up the RNs in Assisted Living. Therefore shortly after I was hired, I was promoted to Med Aid and moved into the Assisted Living side of the Care Center.

Though managed as separate businesses, Assisted Living and long-term care were separated only by legal paperwork and double doors at the end of a short hallway. My work schedule went from 3:00 in the afternoon until 10:00 p.m. Since I had other life and business demands, I could only work at the Center three days per week. While you might think this would be a disadvantage to recognizing particular challenges, it was actually very beneficial because I saw more by stepping away and then stepping back in.

Inexplicably to my DON, I would catch emergencies, critical conditions, and changes in the health of residents that the nursing staff seemed to miss. These changes in condition were pronounced for me, but for some odd reason, they weren't to the rest of the nursing staff.

The response of my DON, when I would call her in the evening to alert her that I would have to send someone to the emergency room, was not, "Great job, Judy, thanks so much, good catch!" Which I think would have been appropriate and appreciated by me, but unfortunately, it was quite the opposite. Her reaction was anger. She was not happy that I was the one who kept spotting critical medical conditions in our residents. Instead, she angrily asked, "Why aren't my nurses catching these things?" It made me wonder if she wasn't taking me seriously or thought perhaps that I was the cause!

She would sternly ask, "Why do *you* keep catching these things?" At first, I was just as dumbfounded. However, sending them to the emergency room was valid and necessary in each situation. And in at least one case, it got back to me that the doctors told the resident that she would not have lived through the night had she not been sent.

But the DON's anger and questions made me take a step back and seriously think about what I was doing differently or what was different about me than the rest of the staff. Serious reflection led me to my first significant "*aha*" moment.

MINDSET: MEASURE OF SUCCESS

As I took that step back and considered the DON's frustration and questions, I noticed what the answers might be. I first noticed that waiting for residents to hit their call light tended to put the nursing staff in a passive response mode, which meant there was a false assumption that if no one was hitting their call light, everything was just fine! Yet, nothing could be farther from the truth.

Since only double doors separated Assisted Living from the long-term care side, many of our Assisted Living residents did not want to press that call light since they feared they would wind up in long-term care. And, of course, they all viewed long-term care as they did the old Eagles song, *Hotel California*, where *you can check out anytime you like, but you can never leave*. Their thinking is, *My next step is a tag on my toe, and then it's off to the Coroner!* Many residents will do anything, including going into denial or trying to accommodate their discomfort, to avoid hitting that call light which can send them out of the independence of Assisted Living and into the more restricted long-term care.

I also recognized that for some of the nursing staff, scheduled tasks seemed to change their measure of success from resident care to being thankful when each task was accomplished. Consider some of the comments I would often hear. "I can't believe I got all my meds passed within the allotted time today." Or, "Wow, with four minutes left, I'm so happy I got everyone fed and in bed!" Can you relate?

Strict time pressures have unwittingly turned much of the nursing staff into clock watchers. However, the reality is that these professionals are in the life-saving business. Though many residents are toward the end of their life, the nursing staff is still in the business of saving lives and increasing the quality of those lives, which is an extremely high calling!

NOT INCOMPETENCE

The training I'm sharing with you throughout this book has absolutely nothing to do with an issue of incompetence. Much of it is simply the nature of the position, the unique environment, and what we do and don't do regarding how new people are trained. Therefore an additional perspective is necessary. Having come into the Care Center as a recently certified CNA, I knew how CNAs were taught and how they viewed their responsibilities and themselves. I was in my late 40s when I attained my certification and became like "Mom" to many young people who went through the course with me. They were very candid about their struggles, both professionally and personally. I understood their mindset, which was consistent with the CNAs I began working with, and I found it very *task-oriented*. The training itself led to that mindset. Consider it for a moment: I brush their teeth, help them dress, toilet them, assist with feeding... I think you get the picture. It was all very *task-oriented*.

CNAs do not see themselves as medical personnel even though they are invaluable to the nursing staff and can and do take basic vitals. The first thing that must happen when training CNAs to become Med Aids, Med Assists, Med Techs, or whichever title is used for the person who administers medications to the residents is to be sure to help them make that vital transition to seeing themselves as *medical personnel*. You must be sure your Med Techs are *medically minded*. You must be sure they understand that their new position holds serious responsibility and consequences. They must not view passing medications as another task on par with dressing, toileting, or feeding.

The importance of this transition gained greater weight when I considered what I experienced with those who went through the Med Tech training with me. I could tell the CNAs were not making a transition in their mind from *task-oriented* to *medically minded*. An emphasis on this for them is vital. To help them transition from seeing the passing of medications as simply another task to being *medically minded*, trainers need to move their trainees slightly beyond the five rights while ensuring the newbie Med Techs remain within their scope of practice, which is possible. I know. I did it without even realizing it!

DON'T KNOCK IT!

To give you an idea of how important it is to ensure the CNAs who promote to the Med Tech position switch from *task* to *medically* minded, I must share with you what I experienced. I recognize that some professionals dismiss anecdotal experiences, but we do this to our detriment. As I have shared these examples from coast to coast since 2018, the reactions and comments from those attending my workshops prove that the same pitfalls are happening across the United States.

I want to preface the following examples by saying I created this training after leaving the Care Center where I worked and that the staff in that particular Care Center was actually the first *LPNequip.org* training I ever conducted. It was a *noodle-against-the-wall* kind of experience. There is considerable risk to creating something and then presenting it to those who once worked with you at a particular level. Yet I could see the "*aha*" moments on their faces and heard from them afterward the positive impact of this training, which propelled me to move *LPNequip.org* forward nationally and now in book form.

To my knowledge, the challenges I state throughout this training were rectified at my previous place of employment after I conducted my *LPNequip.org* training. Since then, they have also experienced turnover from the top down, and that particular Care Center continues to provide high-quality care.

REAL-WORLD EXAMPLES

The following accounts should help you better understand why Med Techs should view themselves as medical personnel and need to be medically minded. I have changed the names of each individual, resident or not, to protect their privacy.

The first example happened with a gentleman named Buddy. Buddy came to my cart as I worked as a Med Tech on the Assisted Living side. He requested a PRN ("*pro re nata*" or "as needed") *Milk of Magnesia*. What I would jokingly refer to as *milk of mag-nausea*.

When defaulting to the typical Med Tech training, what is the first thing drilled into the trainee's mind that they must do before dispensing any PRN medication requested by a resident? Without flinching, I can tell you that what is drilled into the mind of the future Med Tech is that they must check the Medication Administration Record (MAR) *first* to be sure that their resident not only has the medication available to them but has not received the medication within a specific time frame which would allow or disallow them to receive their dose. However, see if you can tell what I did before that step that made a crucial difference.

Upon Buddy's request, I asked, "Are you constipated?"

He chuckled a bit and said, "No."

I then asked, "Do you have a hard stool? Are you just having a hard time going?" (Apologies for the nature of the conversation, but it is what it is!)

To which Buddy responded, "No, quite the opposite!"

I then confirmed, "So you've been having diarrhea?"

Looking at me as if I had lost the plot, Buddy exclaimed, "Well, yeah!" with a tone that would communicate *Dummy, that's why I'm asking you for Milk of Mag!*

I then informed him, "Well, you don't need *Milk of Mag*. Sir, you need *Imodium!*"

Stunned, he asked, "I do?"

I then said, "Well, you bet! Let's look at the MAR and see if you have Imodium, and if you do, let's check when you received your last dose." Sure enough, he did have that medication, and I gave him his dose.

Upon checking on him and asking if it had worked, he said, with great relief, that it had. Mind you, this gentleman had complained of general weakness, was experiencing dizzy spells, and had a few syncope episodes. Eventually, a pole was placed next to his bed so he could easily pull himself up and get out since he had lost strength. It might have been his natural decline, but perhaps something helped in that process when considering what had happened with this gentleman.

When I *looked at the MAR*, what did I see? I saw repeated doses of Milk of Magnesia several times per week. Why? Because it was drilled into the mind of every newly trained Med Tech to *look at the MAR* above and before all else when residents ask for their PRN medications. That's just what they did. What else did they see? They also noticed his PRN Milk of Mag was within the allotted time frame to dispense. Therefore, they would give it to him right on time. Later, when they did their follow-up to see if the medication worked, they would check on him as per protocol. They would then ask, "Did that Milk of Mag work for you?"

Of course, his reply was, "No, it didn't work at all!" Why? Because he knew he still had diarrhea!

Being concerned for what they believed was pretty bad constipation based upon his requests and responses, they would then ask, because it now fell within the allotted time, "Do you want some more?"

To which Buddy would reply, "Sure!"

"Here ya go!" responded the helpful Med Tech as they handed him another dose of the wrong medication. That's right. The wrong medication! Then what do we have? An individual getting completely dehydrated, which we know drops your blood pressure, can make you dizzy and lightheaded, and then *TIMBER!* He'd have a fall. Now I will ask you as I ask my audiences across this country. Is that a medication error? Absolutely! Every single time he got it because it was the wrong medication.

MISS MAISY

Then we come to a very precious lady I will call Maisy. One afternoon when I came to work after having been gone for about four days, I was greeted by a CNA who told me that Maisy was asking for her Tylenol *again*. I said, "What? Not Maisy! You must be mistaken."

I was assured by the CNA, "Yes, Maisy. She's been getting it."

Completely shocked, I confirmed, "She's been getting it? Are you sure?"

"Yes, and she wants some more right now," my coworker urged. I then proceeded to *look at the MAR*. I noticed she had been getting her PRN Tylenol for several days, like clockwork. What you need to know about Maisy is that, because of her religious worldview, she denied the existence of the disease process and sickness and therefore had no assigned medications. However, not thinking Maisy would ever take it, but just in case, her doctor did prescribe a PRN Tylenol for her, which was on the MAR.

I went into Maisy's room holding the Tylenol in my hand, wondering how much pain a person could be in to take their entire religious worldview and set it aside just for a PRN Tylenol. Could she have been at a two out of ten pain level? A five out of ten to receive that? No, I imagined it would have to be pretty severe. Holding it in my hand because I want her to answer me, and she will answer my question to get her Tylenol, I asked, "Maisy, your back hurts you?"

She said, with a grimace on her face, "Oh, yes."

I never heard her complain about her back before, so I confirmed more directly, "Your back hurts you."

She said, "Yes."

I asked, "How long has your back been hurting you?"

She said, "Oh, probably about a week."

I then asked, "Can I see it?" At this juncture, it is important to note that EMS is indeed a naked sport. We will cut your clothes off for a hangnail. *Expose! Expose! Expose!* Perhaps that is a bit of an exaggeration, but as an EMT, I wanted to see *everything*. Sure enough, Maisy lowered the back of her slacks, and to my horror, she had severe shingles. Yes, she was in a lot of pain. She also should not have been walking around our Care Center!

She then coyly confessed, "My legs hurt too."

I said, "Your legs hurt too?" I always repeat what they tell me back to them because sometimes they get more specific. Usually, when I repeat it back, the response I hear will be, "Actually, it's really just my knee."

Not this time! Maisy said, "Yes, my legs hurt me."

To which I asked (you guessed it), "Can I see it?" This poor woman had pitting edema from her feet to well above her knees. She was shipped out to the emergency room and never returned to Assisted Living but remained in the long-term care side of our Care Center from that point on.

MISS GERTIE

Then we have a resident whom I will call Gertie. Once again, I had been gone for about four days, returned, and was immediately met by the receptionist who said Gertie had been asking for her narcotic pain medication. Once again, I queried, "Gertie? What's wrong with Gertie?"

"Her arm still hurts her," I was told matter-of-factly.

In three years, Gertie had never requested a narcotic pain reliever from me. She didn't particularly like taking any medications. As I looked in the MAR, sure enough, it showed that she had been taking it for the entire time I was gone. It seemed odd to see the notation in the MAR stating that she requested it for arm pain without further explanation. *Arm pain?* I thought to myself as I went to her room. *What is with this arm pain?* I never knew her to complain about having trouble with her arm before.

As I entered her room, she was relaxing in her bed, and I asked, "Gertie, your arm is hurting you?"

She said, "Yes."

Changing my vocal tone slightly, I confirmed, "Your arm is hurting you." Making it more like a statement.

She then said, "Well, actually, it's my elbow."

I asked, "Okay, how long has your *elbow* been hurting you?"

She thought for a moment and then stated, "Since Sunday."

"Sunday?" I queried further, "Well, what happened this last Sunday that suddenly, out of the blue, your arm started hurting you?"

She said very casually, "I fell against the door."

Stunned, I said, "You fell against the door! Did you tell anybody?"

She began laughing as she said, "No. In fact, you're the first person to ask!" We then had her elbow x-rayed and found that she had unfortunately fractured it. Yes, Gertie's arm hurt her very much. Was she eager to tell us why or how? She never offered. Therefore there are a few things to do and consider before we *look at the MAR.*

THE DANGER OF SEMANTICS

Before I cover the steps in our next chapter that should be taken before *looking at the MAR*, I want to touch upon something I also noticed that could unwittingly decrease the quality of care for our residents.

When I went through the course to attain my CNA credential, what was drilled into our minds was that we were to refer to those we care for as *residents* or *clients* and *NOT* as patients. Since I was also an EMT, now and again, I would slip and refer to them as *patients*. And oh, the rebuke I received!

Please don't misunderstand me on this point. I fully understand and agree with the reasoning for referring to those in your care as residents or clients. When someone in your care is referred to as a *resident* or *client*, it implies a sense of independence, it implies competence, and it also gives them the appropriate sense that the people who work there are working for them. If I were in a Care Center, referring to me as a resident or client would make me feel better. While I understand why that is done and how important it is for residents or clients to feel as independent and competent as possible, a step back and rethinking into how and why we train on this should be taken.

For example, when we lived in an apartment, as my husband and I waited for our home to be built, our landlord never came and passed our medications to us. Why? Because we were, in actuality, *residents*.

We must understand, though, that the individuals served in Assisted Living and long-term care facilities are there for medical reasons. Their complaints are medical in nature. When they decline, it is because of medical conditions. Therefore, they must be viewed as patients, and the nursing staff must regard themselves as responsible for their care in various ways, especially medically.

I wholeheartedly agree with referring to them as residents or clients when *talking* with them. Still, the mindset must be that you serve patients who can be fragile, whose conditions can change. Since their conditions can change, so can their cognition and understanding of their PRN medications. They can then become confused and thus request *Milk of Mag* rather than *Imodium*. Since dispensing the proper medication is paramount to avoiding medication errors that can harm the residents or worse, there is a duty that even if *they* are confused, those who pass medications at your Center won't be.

In the next chapter, I will provide more help by showing you questions to ask residents that do indeed fall within the scope of practice for nursing.

QUESTIONS FOR THOUGHT

1) Are there areas in your Care Center where the training imparted in this chapter could make a difference?
2) If you are being trained as a Med Tech, do you see the importance of shifting how you view passing medications?
3) What is it about passing medications that takes it out of the realm of simply another task?
4) If you are a DON, administrator, or owner, would it make sense to retrain in some areas for a fuller perspective on the CNA/Med Tech position?
5) Are your LPNs and RNs asking the right questions as well?

2. Training Misses and Commonsense Fixes

What I will impart to you throughout this chapter is not beyond the scope of practice for nursing staff. I fully understand concerns about having a person who holds EMS credentials and then decides to train in nursing. However, what I'm going to put forth falls perfectly in line with those who administer medications and other staff members who perhaps can recognize that something might be off with a resident but, with this training, can have the ability to alert medical staff. The information in this chapter will help caregivers to be more effective, help them feel more successful in their position, increase the quality of the residents' healthcare, and save lives.

RAPID ASSESSMENTS

When I took a step back to try to understand the differences between EMS and nursing, what I was doing differently than what my co-workers were doing (or not doing), I realized that a significant key was that without ever being conscious of it, I was consistently in *rapid assessment* mode. Think about this for a moment. As a volunteer First Responder and EMS provider, I respond from home to the fire station or directly to the incident scene. A significant responsibility, especially if I am first on the scene, is to report what I witness with my patient to the responding medic unit or ambulance as soon as possible, allowing them to be better prepared for the call. Therefore my rapid assessments happened as soon as I walked through the patient's door.

As a matter of practice, I was constantly assessing individuals. I would observe them, looking for signs and listening to them describe symptoms as I asked questions regarding their health. And since rapid assessments were to happen as soon as I laid eyes on a patient as an EMT, without realizing it, I carried on the habit of rapidly assessing when I gave my residents their medications in Assisted Living.

However, something I added made rapid assessments more effective for me and more fun for my residents. I ensured that my baseline when my client saw me was always upbeat, no matter what mood I was in. It was important for me to leave whatever baggage or lousy day I had at the front door of the Care Center. (More on this in a later chapter.)

GETTING A BASELINE

I have a pretty good sense of humor and even engaged in stand-up comedy many years ago. Usually, I would say something funny to my resident, yet not inappropriate. If it were raining hard, I might say, "I'm so glad I had the opportunity to swim here today," then my resident would begin to chuckle. I had one resident, whom I will call Ed, who was so used to me coming into his room with something humorous that his baseline whenever I saw him was to lean forward toward me as he smiled wide with an anticipatory expression as if to say, *Here comes Funny!*

One afternoon I entered Ed's room and immediately noticed that he was not at his personal baseline. His posture was very stiff as he sat straight up. His arms were on the arms of his chair as his fingers clenched the ends. His eyes were wide open, and his skin color was ashen. Concerned, I asked, "Ed, what's wrong?"

Ed immediately said, "I can't breathe."

Did he pull the call light? Nope. Remember that *Hotel California* kind of thinking? Some would rather die than go to *the other side* in long-term care. Wanting to calm his fears, I told Ed that he had enough air to keep alive if he could talk. I did an assessment, and his oxygen saturation levels were pretty low. Therefore, we immediately sent him to the emergency room.

With this in mind, when we walk through the door of our resident's room in Assisted Living or elsewhere, we must note if they are alert. Are they oriented? Do they know where they are and who you are? What is their posture? Knowing the baseline for each person you serve or how they usually respond when you walk through the door lets you know if something isn't right.

COUNTENANCE

Another thing to assess for is their countenance or facial expression. In the evenings, all my residents always watched the same two programs. You guessed it, *Wheel of Fortune* and *Jeopardy*. One night I walked into Anna's room. She did not have *Wheel Of Fortune* or *Jeopardy* on her television, per usual. To my surprise, her television was off, and she was staring into space with her back to it. This behavior was not her baseline.

Troubled, I got close to Anna, bent down, put my hands on my knees, looked into her eyes, and asked, "Anna, what's wrong?" I then firmly held to the old sales axiom *She who talks first, loses*. I don't peep, I don't change my expression, and I don't take my eyes off of them until they answer my question. My residents knew I was stubborn and would wait for their answer because they knew I was serious about their response. It always worked!

Anna said, "Well, my son got into another fight with his wife." I could see by her expression that it was weighing on her.

I replied gently, "It sounds like they've had fights in the past."

She said, "Yes."

I said, "Well, it sounds like they've patched things up because they're still together. You do realize that the fun part is the making up?" Anna chuckled a little bit. Then I said, "Since they've patched it up in the past, I'm pretty sure they'll patch it up again. And, oh my goodness, how much fun it is to make up!" Anna began to giggle. I suggested, "How about we pop on Wheel of Fortune and see if Pat Sajak will finally fall into the wheel when he gives it a spin."

The good news was that I left her in a better emotional place than before I entered her room. And that should always be our goal no matter who we encounter. As caregivers, that is a pretty big deal.

However, what if I went into Anna's room and asked the *what's wrong* question, and she replied, "Well, I'm just getting so tired of being treated like a little kid where somebody has to hand me my medications and tell me when to eat, what to eat, where I can go, and when I can go. My children never visit me as they tell me they hate these places, but it's perfectly okay that they stuck me here. I'm in chronic pain, and I'll tell you honestly, I hate this place too, and I can't see any more reason to keep taking not only those stinking medications but food and water as well!" If this were Anna's response, that would be of great concern, and I should notify the DON or Administrator for them to take it from there. Yet, if I were the harried and hurried Med Tech, I would never know the level of her despair since I would be too busy watching the clock since my only concern would be, *How fast can I finish this med pass and clock out so I don't get in trouble for overtime?*

We have lost a vital skill in our society that puts us at a disadvantage regarding rapid assessment. It affects our ability to spot something happening with our residents. We see people, but we don't look at them. Our constant gazing at devices just might be putting us at a disadvantage when looking at people. We don't make eye contact anymore. The fact is your residents are constantly changing. Some changes are subtle, some not so much. But your nursing staff will miss them all if they don't look to assess as soon as they see them.

SKIN COLOR/QUALITY

Upon entering a resident's room, I rapidly assessed their body language, countenance, skin color, and quality. I will never forget entering Mabel's room, and to my shock, I immediately noticed that she was cyanotic! She was white as a ghost, her lips and nails were a lovely shade of blue, and I'm not talking about lipstick or matching nail polish!

Mabel was also quite lethargic; again, people had been in and out of her room throughout the day. Now what I needed to remember about Mabel was that she took very high doses of pain medication. Whatever PRN pain meds Mabel could receive, she got at precisely the time she was able. She never missed one. What happens when people are on high doses of pain medications? It can depress their breathing. When I assessed her, her oxygen saturation level was in the mid-70s. I could not believe she was even conversing with me in that condition. She was immediately sent to the emergency room, and when she returned, she thanked us and told us that we had saved her life by catching her condition in time.

GUARDING & GAIT

Guarding was something else I observed with my residents who aren't too keen about admitting when they are hurting. Are they protecting an area on their body that they never had before? What I noticed about Gertie, the resident with the fractured elbow, was that she held it whenever she went into the dining room as if to communicate to others, *Please don't bump into this!* If you notice guarding in one of your residents, simply walk up to the individual and ask, "I notice you're protecting your elbow, is everything okay?"

Again residents don't always state when something is wrong, but we sure need to perk up our ears when they do. I will never forget coming into work one day, and as I looked down the hallway with my coat still on and purse still on my shoulder, I noticed something troubling in one of my residents. He was walking toward me, his gait was off, and he had an agitated expression. I immediately approached him, asking, "Gary, what's wrong?"

He said, "I don't know, I don't feel right, and I'm scared." His expression of fear was very out of character for him. Also, take it seriously when a resident tells you they are scared! As the saying goes, *the living know they must die*. They have a sense before we do. An individual can look perfectly okay, but I immediately assess when anyone tells me this. This bit of intuitiveness, I have found over the years, winds up being reasonably accurate.

I asked Gary, "When did you start feeling bad?"

Gary said, "Since lunch."

I asked, "Did you tell anybody?"

He said, "Yes, I did. But they said I was just hungry."

No one assessed Gary after he ate. Unfortunately, he had had a stroke. My catching his condition at 3:00 in the afternoon meant we missed that all-important *Golden Hour* for stroke patients. Again, we must train staff to be more alert to these situations. When they catch these particular conditions, they feel more confident and successful working at your Care Center because they see their impact on the lives of those who are in their care.

ASSESSMENT PARTICULARS

Any person responsible for administering medications to a patient is trained on the *five rights*. Though we do realize there are six:

1. The right medication.
2. The right patient.
3. The right dose.
4. The right route.
5. The right time.
6. The right expiration date.

When I became a Med Tech, I was also trained on the five steps to medication administration:

1. Evaluating the patient.
2. Setting up the medication.
3. Administering the medication.
4. Documentation.
5. Observing the patient.

The two essential steps that place rapid assessments within nursing's scope of practice are #1 and #5. Evaluating the patient before administering the medication and then observing the success or failure of that medication is a perfect fit for what I am stressing as essential steps to not only passing medications but, as a rule, when working in a care facility. A habit of rapidly assessing the residents at your Care Center should flow naturally for the observant caregiver or staff member.

OPQRST

Borrowing from my EMS training, there are some key questions to ask that help gain a little ground in answering the "*What's wrong?*" question you will pose to your residents or when conducting Step #1 for evaluating and Step #5 for your observation. As an EMT, I found the acronym *OPQRST* which I learned during my initial training, quite helpful and easy to remember for gaining information regarding my patient's and residents' conditions. With the information given to you by the resident, each element can be included in the chart, passed onto a doctor, or described to a 9-1-1 dispatcher. They are as follows:

O = ONSET: "What triggered your pain, nausea, dizziness, fatigue… ?" Here, you would ask what the patient believes brought on their condition change or what happened to start this change of condition or injury. Perhaps they would tell you their pain began after falling against a door! Or maybe the onset of their symptoms started after eating the bean burrito or candy their family member brought them. They might even state that it was a dull ache that intensified as time went on.

P = PROVOKES: "What causes you to hurt more?" Or, "What causes you to, or when do you become dizzy?" It is helpful to know what aggravates the condition more or less because you would want to place your resident in a position of comfort. It is also beneficial to alert other caregivers so that when they're dressing the individual, they know that this is a new condition that needs special care. Depending upon what they state provokes the pain or aggravates their symptoms might also alert us to a more severe condition.

Q = QUALITY: "How would you describe your pain?" Be sure to get a clear description of the discomfort from the resident. Do they describe the pain as sharp, throbbing, a dull ache, or perhaps a tearing pain? If they state that they feel a tearing pain in their stomach, could this be an *abdominal aortic aneurysm*? If so, since this is a life-threatening condition, we would absolutely want to know.

R = RADIATE: "Where did you first feel this pain, and where does your pain go?" If they say it's in their left arm and up into their jaw, could this be their heart? Do they state that the pain began in their tummy and then traveled to their lower right side? Perhaps it's their appendix. We won't know if we don't ask.

S = SEVERITY: "On a scale of one to ten, how high is your pain?" Many caregivers realize that asking a resident their thoughts on the pain scale can be tricky. Some residents fear the one dispensing the medication won't give them enough to help relieve their pain. Therefore, some might calmly shrug as they respond that they are at a *ten out of ten*. As caregivers, we realize that we never really have to ask anyone if they are at a ten out of ten pain level. As a First Responder, I can hear them upon my approach. Usually, I will ask, "On a scale of one to ten, I know you're not at a one because you're uncomfortable enough to want medication, but I also know you're probably not at a ten because you're not screaming, so realistically where is your pain level?" Posed in this way, it usually prompts them to think about it a bit more before answering. I also explain that an accurate answer will help us to give them a proper dose.

T = TIME: "How long has this been hurting, concerning, or bothering you?" Don't simply look at the MAR and assume it started hurting them upon the first day they took pain medications. Their pain or condition might have been brewing for a while, which is important.

As you look back at that list of questions, please don't be concerned that posing them might take longer than usual, especially considering how long it takes to tend to a resident and the paperwork afterward if someone falls due to dehydration or hypoxia. The issue of time should not be a driving concern. The concern should be, *Am I providing the best in quality care? Am I encouraging my caregivers to succeed in their role as effective medical personnel?*

WHO'S TRAINING THE NEWBIES?

As someone who came to nursing *bright-eyed and bushy-tailed*, I was like a sponge whenever any training opportunities came my way. I wanted to glean all I could to be the best I could be at my Care Center with my residents. It was my natural inclination as someone with a high-level customer service attitude to be sure that's just what they received. If it were drilled into my head that these were clients, I would treat them with the highest level of customer service they could expect. With every training opportunity I received, I took it seriously and with great anticipation.

However, I know the approach to the training I received is not unusual in Care Centers throughout the United States. And again, as I conduct my *LPNequip.org* training across the country, the confirmation remains the same. When management attains a new hire, especially a CNA or Med Tech, they look for who is available on the floor to fulfill the training duties. Unfortunately, availability does not necessarily mean an individual will be an effective trainer. Such was the case for me.

When I began working on the long-term care side of the Care Center, which also included hospice patients and those who stayed there on a short-term basis for rehabilitation, I was yoked to a different person each day as a new hire and a recent CNA graduate. Some were eager to teach. Others were not. Most viewed it as a nuisance to have someone shadowing them and throwing them off their usual beat. Remember what I shared regarding the clock-watcher mindset? Well, since I was the one who threw them off, sometimes I would feel their subtle displeasure. Throughout most of that time, I felt like the annoying little sister following big sister or brother as I asked, "Can I try?" or "Can I see how you did that?"

There are some pitfalls to simply grabbing someone available on the floor and yoking them to the newbie. There will be missing details with each generation because there is significant turnover within nursing, especially at the CNA level. So even if you find the most senior person, depending upon the shift, that person might only have been there for six months. I was stunned to hear that most of the people I shadowed had only been there a matter of months, yet they were in a vital training role. Unfortunately, the amount of turnover did not allow for more experienced individuals to pass on their knowledge to me. Many "trainers" wanted to get in, get on with it, and get out of there as fast as possible.

Like most people in our society, I saw a lot of *hurry sickness*. There were pitfalls to that. Since we tend to mimic our trainers, it's easy to pass a negative or clock-watcher mentality on to the newbie. And the accounts below will show lessons to learn that remind caregivers to slow down a bit and take a minute or two extra with our residents, or they will miss why they do their job in the first place.

RHONDA

As I followed my trainer from room to room on the long-term care side, one of the residents I served I will call Rhonda. I found her quite intriguing. With a quiet voice, I could hear her talking very swiftly. She seemed agitated but still allowed us to do what we needed to do with her as if we weren't there. The person training me that day could tell I was straining a little bit to listen to what she was saying. I was then told starkly, "Oh, don't worry about what she's saying. She babbles like that constantly. Just ignore it. We need to move on." *Got it!*

Rhonda's clothes were very stylish, and her jewelry, though costume, was high-end. Bits and pieces of what she would say sounded familiar to me, making me curious. When I was finally on my own, and after about a month of caring for Rhonda and attempting to understand her a bit more, her sister happened to be in her room one day. I asked her sister if Rhonda had any particular occupation. Her sister's eyes raised as she seemed happy to tell me more about Rhonda. She stated that her sister had been in real estate but not homes in neighborhoods. She noted that Rhoda was a real estate agent for commercial buildings and had conducted multi-million dollar deals. I nodded as some of what she would "babble" now made sense.

One day as I was feeding Rhonda during the dinner hour, some of what she was saying began to click, so I asked, "Rhonda, are you working on a deal right now?"

She looked directly at me for the first time in the months I had cared for her. She said in her quick yet quiet voice but with a serious expression, "Yes, I'm doing a very important deal. This is San Francisco, and we need to get this done." Actually, it was Washington State in a Care Center, but that didn't matter to me! We had made a connection. Suddenly, we had a mini conversation, and I thought it was beautiful. It was in Rhonda's world, but that connection meant a lot. My *conversation* with Rhonda made me more aware of my service to her. It made it more personal. Had I listened to my *trainer*, would I even bother asking Rhonda's sister questions? Would I have taken that extra time to understand her better? Would we have made any connection?

FRED

Then there was Fred. During training, I was told that Fred had a massive stroke, couldn't speak or respond, and was probably unaware of what was happening around him. I was told that *we do everything for Fred* and to just go in, get it done, and get out of there. One evening, about three months into my care for him, I noticed an audio tape player in his room. I said, "Fred, you have audio tapes here. Perhaps you would like to listen to one." So I popped one in, and it began to play a beautiful old hymn. I stood at his dresser, looking at the player as he lay on his bed behind me. I said, "Oh, Fred, I love this song. I haven't heard it in years. I love this!"

From behind me, I heard a low voice speak the words, "I do too."

Though stunned, I casually walked over to Fred as he lay there, crouched down, and said, "You love this song too?"

To which he replied, "Yes, it's my favorite."

I asked, "Fred, would you like me to play tapes for you in the evenings that I'm working?"

He said, "Yes, that would be very nice."

One evening at dinner, I noticed a cat run through the little courtyard area we could see from the windows. And I said, "Oh, Fred, there's a cat right there!"

To which he responded, "That cat is there every day."

I had no idea how long Fred had been at the Care Center before I arrived or if he had ever spoken to anyone else. It certainly didn't seem like it. But it indeed was a lesson for me! One that I hope is a lesson you can pass on to those who work with you. Let's remember these are people with needs that are not just physical. It just takes a bit of time and trust to draw them out. The enduring caregiver, whom the patient can trust, will do just that.

MENTORING

When it comes to training, we need people willing to be trained and then engage in mentoring. As you think about the CNAs who work at your Center, ask yourself, *Who is the best*? Remember that the one who gets in the room and out the quickest isn't necessarily the one who would fulfill that requirement as being *the best*. Sometimes they get the job done fast for all the wrong reasons, and if you asked other CNAs who work with them, they would confirm it. Many times there are shortcuts made in essential areas that can impact the health of your residents.

Sometimes your best employee isn't necessarily the best person to train. Perhaps they're not good at mentoring or explaining what they're doing. I had to *shadow* someone like that. They were very good at their job but didn't know how to transfer or communicate that talent.

We need to train trainers on how we want things done to streamline as much as possible. It always made me sad when I came to the Care Center and would hear what seemed like a compliment but was heartbreaking. After a sigh of relief, the comment most expressed to me was, "Oh, I'm so glad it's you working today!" Why did they say that? Because each caregiver or Med Tech did things differently. And apparently, those differences didn't always meet the resident's particular needs.

MENTOR TRAINER

The added role of a *mentor* should be treated as special. We should not forget that having a new hire shadowing an employee is an inconvenience for them throughout their day. It slows them down. The one mentoring and training is constantly interrupted by being asked and then answering questions or demonstrating tasks. Therefore, I suggest your center gives the individual you select to streamline how you want that particular job accomplished, and this goes for any position in the workplace, the title of *Mentor Trainer*, as you also offer a financial bonus for each new hire they train. It doesn't have to be a raise in salary because they are not constantly training. But when they do, a little extra cash as a thank-you helps them take the position more seriously, boosts their morale, helps them feel more responsible for the new individual, and certainly takes the sting out of the inconvenience.

And again, having one individual on each shift training and mentoring new staff allows more efficiency and consistency for the residents. After the new hire is trained, be sure to have them evaluate their *Mentor Trainer*. The trainer should know they will be evaluated. The evaluations will expose any adjustments you need to make in the duties they are imparting, whether the *Mentor Trainer* needs more training or if that leadership position isn't a right fit for the mentor you selected.

"THE LIVING DEAD?"

Not only was I a *shadow* in long-term care as a CNA, but I also found myself again in that position when promoted to Med Tech in Assisted Living. When my first day came for training on the medication cart as a newbie, I could not have been more eager to learn as much as possible from the nurse I was instructed to shadow. I have always admired and respected those in nursing and nurses in particular. As the POA for a loved one in a long-term care facility for ten years, I recognized that they did things to help strangers that few people were willing to do. I watched with admiration at the tenderness many expressed toward their residents. EMS and nursing could benefit significantly from each other's unique training and experiences.

Perhaps it was because I cared for my grandmother as she was ailing or because of Clarence, the loved one for whom I was the POA (more on him in a later chapter). Perhaps it was my walk-in-their-shoes mindset or desire to provide high-level customer service as a throwback to my corporate sales years. Whatever prompted it, I was and remain a stickler regarding the dignity of those I serve, whether patients, residents, or ailing loved ones. So what happened on my first day on the cart as a Med Tech upon meeting the nurse who would train me burned into my heart and memory.

Though my schedule would be the evening shift, I would train as a Med Tech during the busiest med pass—the first thing in the morning. I was excited to meet the nurse who would show me the ropes. I knew she was retiring and felt very honored to glean from her years of experience. I had so many questions. As I eagerly awaited, the Assisted Living nurse walked into the room, where I was greeted with a grunt and a nod. She put her hand up as if to stop any words from coming out of my mouth until she sipped coffee. Her first words to me were, "Give me a minute." I quietly complied. She took off her coat and set her things aside in our small office on the Assisted Living side of the Care Center. With a heavy sigh, she asked in bewilderment, "So you wanted to be a Med Tech?"

A bit confused, as the air slowly exited my bubble, I hesitantly replied, "Well, I'd like to give it a shot." That was all she asked about me, and that was all I offered. In uncomfortable silence, we set up for the morning med pass.

When we finished prepping, she looked at me and said, in a tone dripping with sarcasm, "Are you ready for *Night of the Living Dead*?"

Confused, I said, "Excuse me?"

With an exasperated attitude and a monotone voice, she stated, "Just wait. They're here every morning."

As we opened the door, my eyes beheld hurting residents walking toward us as quickly as possible to receive their needed pain medication. It felt like a swift kick in the gut when I realized that the woman I would shadow for the next month referred to human beings who relied on us to help get them out of pain. I had been so excited to finally train in this new position with someone in a field I so respected, only to have my first impression be of a trainer dripping with contempt for those she was supposed to serve.

Imagine, for a moment, the impact she would have had on me if she had said, "Hi Judy, it's great to meet you. Congrats on your new medical position. I'm so pleased to be working with you. I need to give you a head's up with the morning med pass. Many of our residents will take their meds in the evening, and by the morning, they are in so much pain that even though they are at a high level, they walk down and wait outside the door each morning to be first to receive it. So please be sure you start your med pass on time so we can help our residents with their pain." If this were how things went, I imagine it would prompt compassion in my heart passed on to me from the one who trained me. It would cause me to pause and see them as hurting individuals I can help. It would make me feel good that I could do that for them. Her kindness would make me proud and cause me to stay in such an impactful field and Care Center.

People generally mimic their teachers. Bad attitudes rub off more easily than good ones. Pulling someone off a platform is far easier than lifting someone onto one. Can you imagine how miserable it would be if I were a different person and mimicked my trainer by opening the door each morning, viewing human beings as *Night of the Living Dead?* How horrible would that be, and how long would I want that career? I was thrilled she was retiring. What an awful first impression. Note to all who hire: perhaps the burned-out retiring nurse shouldn't be the one who trains the excited, thankful, eager newbies!

THE REALITY OF CHANGING STAFF

I noticed something else that can put pressure on specific individuals within Care Centers, causing them to feel uncomfortable and unsuccessful. Some individuals have worked there for a long time and want to stay on since they have a wealth of experience to pass on to others. These are individuals who might make great mentors. I'm talking about our older caregivers.

In the Assisted Living where I worked, there were two women in their sixties and one in her seventies who I always said I hoped to be when I grew up. But we must ask ourselves if our residents can change over time, can our staff as well? Can everyone hear well enough to check a blood pressure or hear lung sounds? Can everyone kneel on the floor to aid in a fall or do CPR if there is no DNR?

I remember one instance where one of the older women I worked with wasn't completely honest about her inability to hear as well as she used to when measuring a resident's blood pressure. Her inability gravely impacted one of our residents, who was always energetic and talkative, yet suddenly didn't want to leave her room and kept requesting a room tray. She was sleeping more than usual, and her blood pressure kept coming back normal to high when this particular individual took it. This seemed odd, so my DON looked at me directly and said, "You take it."

When I took the women's blood pressure, it turned out to be very low, so we sent her to the emergency room. Unfortunately, she had pneumonia, and shortly after that, she passed on. Am I blaming that caregiver for her death? Certainly not, but knowing an accurate reading might have meant better care sooner.

Another instance happened when one of my residents had a traumatic injury fall. I held her head to keep her cervical spine (C-spine) in line because she complained of neck pain and because of the nature of her fall. When I asked one of the older CNAs to please take vitals, she looked at the floor and said, "I can't get down there and do that." She then found someone in long-term care who could, which obviously took more time.

Because of the above concerns, we should help staff members, including older caregivers, feel more comfortable communicating their strengths and weaknesses. The fact is that for many who work full-time, they are with their coworkers more than with family. Since this is the case, perhaps it is time to behave as a family and help each other by pairing specific individuals with those who can assist them in various situations. It might make more sense to accommodate older caregivers rather than to encourage them toward retirement if their work ethic is reliable and their vast experience positively influences your center. But you won't know this is happening unless you observe them, ask questions, test them, and follow up.

CONFABULATION FRUSTRATION

There are many conditions that we can consider that seem puzzling, frustrating, and downright difficult to handle as healthcare workers. *Confabulation* is a condition that definitely falls in that realm. People who confabulate are not lying. The fact is, everyone confabulates. We find this all the time with eyewitness testimony. One individual will promise up and down that a perpetrator was wearing blue slacks when they were really wearing beige slacks. Confabulation happens when the mind fills in what the memory can't. This is why, when you have two supposed eyewitnesses, and their testimony is word-for-word, they are more likely to be engaged in collusion.

As caregivers, many of us have had residents who suffered or are suffering from *Korsakoff Syndrome*, which involves confusion, memory challenges, and, you guessed it, *confabulation*. It is fantastic to me the various scenarios folks confabulate. This condition is challenging for caregivers because the individual is not lying. What they confabulate is, to them, absolute truth. It is their reality. It is, to them, a memory. Therefore it is nearly impossible to talk someone out of what they confabulate, which can be pretty tricky for caregivers, especially the hurried ones!

While working in long-term care, I had a resident who would confabulate a whole espionage scenario that he believed was happening at the Care Center, which made him quite paranoid. He genuinely believed that his room was *bugged*. When he told me this, I listened attentively, and with a serious tone, I said, "Okay, what I want you to do is wait right here by your door, and I'm going to do a sweep." I walked around his bed and bathroom, then came to the door where he stood and assured him, "You're all good!" He thanked me very much and went off to bed without a hitch. This event continued every night I worked in long-term care with him as my resident. My job, I felt, was not to talk him out of it because I knew I never would but to let him know everything was okay and that he could go to bed in peace. It took me two minutes.

Then one night, he was met with a hurried caregiver who would not buy into his confabulated stories about listening devices in his room or espionage among the staff. Instead of giving him peace which was what he needed, she argued with him to the point where he lost his temper and wound up punching a mannequin Santa Claus that the Care Center had sitting on a bench near his room. I immediately alerted those at the nurse's station when I saw his outburst and the physical contact he made. "Hey, he just hit Santa!" I alerted.

To which they all laughed. I said, "No, he hit Santa!" with more urgency in my voice. Once again, they started laughing. I said, "You guys, it's not funny. You're not getting it. He made a connection which means if he made a connection with that stuffed Santa, he's going to make a connection with one of us!"

I was scolded, "Oh, Judy, you're being overdramatic! He's fine." And yet that following weekend, while I was gone, he threw a trash can at a caregiver and connected with his fist. He was taken out of there and never returned.

Confabulation is no laughing matter. Part of our job is to help give people the peace they need. And if it takes us a moment to walk around the room to look for an imaginary listening device, so be it. It's far better to do that than to stomp a foot and escalate it because I'm right, they're wrong, I need to tell them that, and I'm in a hurry, resulting in a mound of paperwork, drama, and frustration for the client and the caregiver.

THE #1 COMPLAINT

Before I bring this chapter to a close, if you are in a leadership position at your Care Center, I think it is imperative to address the number one frustration I hear from Assisted Living nursing staff. It is the most consistent complaint I hear as I share my training nationwide. It is when a Care Center has residents who are more appropriate for long-term care but are placed into Assisted Living. I cannot tell you how many caregivers nationwide point this out as their biggest complaint.

Suppose this is the case at your Care Center. If so, you need to realize that daily, your nursing staff is faced with frustration and discouragement because they understand that they, unfortunately, have to neglect their Assisted Living appropriate residents to attempt to meet the needs of individuals more suitable for long-term care. They also understand that there is no way they can fully meet the needs of long-term care individuals in Assisted Living.

Perhaps you have some excellent caregivers who need a break from the physicality of long-term care, and working in Assisted Living makes more sense for them. Therefore, they have made that change only to find the work just as physically demanding yet ultimately unfulfilling. Your staff risks injury if proper lifting equipment is unavailable in Assisted Living when lifting someone who should be in long-term care.

If your Center has long-term care appropriate individuals in Assisted Living, know you will lose good people and neglect not only the Assisted Living residents but also those who need long-term care. What happens in this instance? No one is happy, not the staff or the residents. And what I can ensure will happen is that your nursing staff will begin talking to others who work at Care Centers in your area as they ask, "Do you have long-term care appropriate people in your Assisted Living? Is everybody ambulatory?" And if the answer is "No," to the first question and "Yes," to the second, you can lose good people, and there spins that dreaded revolving door.

QUESTIONS FOR THOUGHT

1) What has worked regarding training at your Care Center? What have you found that has not worked?
2) Are there changes you made once challenges came to your attention? How did you help staff members respond to changes, if any?
3) When do *rapid assessments* happen?
4) How can a trainer with a negative attitude affect a new hire?
5) What are the dangers of hurry sickness? What invaluable moments might be missed in your Care Center?

3. Emergency Situations and EMS Interface

For this short chapter, I will offer some thoughts on the interface between the staff in your Care Center and EMS. I would also like to address particular emergencies and how they can be managed more smoothly. As I worked in both Assisted Living and long-term care, I recognized that not everyone worked well under the pressure of a traumatic injury emergency. I was accustomed to the chaos surrounding a traumatic injury, but some of the nursing staff weren't. For good reason!

If you have a rehabilitation facility within your Center, the staff is accustomed to seeing individuals *after* they have had treatment for a traumatic injury. Rehab, long-term care, hospice, and Assisted Living are not environments where copious amounts of blood or obvious physical deformities from a sudden fall occur regularly with your beloved resident. Keeping yourself and your residents calm remains vital. Remember, other residents and family members can observe your reaction. They might judge your response, which will give them peace or terror if they imagine themselves or a loved one in the same situation.

WORKING WITH EMS

I cannot stress enough that everyone should follow their center's procedures and protocols. However, I have noticed that quality care can be hindered because stringent regulations can cause added liability fears on the part of leadership. For example, one night, while on a break as a Med Tech, I strolled through the double doors to the long-term care side to chat with one of the nurses who was moving on from the Care Center, and it happened to be her last night. As I wished her well, a panicked CNA screamed, "Rosa fell, Rosa fell!"

I went into the front room, where the unwitnessed fall occurred. However, the mechanism of injury was apparent. There was a bookshelf next to her, and it was evident by her injuries that her face had hit each shelf on her way down, shattering one of her eye sockets. She had clotted blood in her mouth and nose, meaning she had been there for a little while. I immediately cleared her airway of the clotted blood and kept her as calm as possible as she lay there, very confused.

Understanding that the mechanism of injury would have snapped Rosa's head back repeatedly, I held her head in line with her spine, or what we refer to in EMS as *holding C-spine*. The Charge Nurse stated that she would call 9-1-1. I urgently said, "Please be sure to tell them C-spine precautions are being taken!"

The Charge Nurse stopped, looked at me, and stated, "I can't, I can't! That's diagnosing!"

I implored, "It's okay, it isn't. Please tell the 9-1-1 dispatcher that C-spine precautions are being taken!"

Throwing up her hand, she replied, "Nope, can't do that," and then left to make the call. In most communities, when 9-1-1 is contacted, the first to respond ahead of the medic unit is the fire department. Unfortunately, in this instance, there had been a significant accident on the freeway, and the only available apparatus they had to send was a brush truck. While a brush truck is excellent for a wildland fire, it doesn't usually have equipment for a traumatic injury fall. Therefore, the firefighters walked in, looked at me, and said, "Oh, you're holding C-spine."

I said, "Yes, I am!"

They then said, "I wish somebody had told us."

I wished the Charge Nurse had told 9-1-1 C-spine precautions were in place as well because we had to wait another forty minutes until the medic unit arrived where they could take over since the whole purpose is to keep their head as still as possible. You don't pass it off to someone else until their head is secured on a backboard. Had they told the 9-1-1 operator that C-spine precautions were in place, the dispatcher would have told the responding unit this information. Then at the fire station, they would have grabbed a backboard, a cervical collar, spider straps, and everything needed to have her packaged. When the medic unit arrived, all that would need to be done would be to pass her off onto a gurney so she would be transported immediately (what EMS refers to as a *load-and-go*) instead of starting that process forty minutes later.

It is perfectly okay to offer a picture of what is or has happened by saying you have *a high index of suspicion* for whatever traumatic injury it might be or whatever medical condition you think the resident might have. Offering this information is not diagnosing. What it does is allow for better care. As you provide information to dispatch, they pass it on to the ambulance in real-time. The paramedics then understand what they need to bring in with them from their unit and can plan who will do what before they even walk through your door.

The information you communicate to the 9-1-1 dispatcher is vital for pre-planning because you want the medics to move quickly and effectively during a medical emergency. They want to as well. It's okay if it turns out to be something else, but at least the EMS personnel have a direction. The paramedics understand that you do not have X-ray vision, but you do have medical knowledge. Please pass that on!

Also, ensure your nursing staff gets a complete set of baseline vitals as soon as possible. Vitals are vital! They are a window to what is happening inside an individual. You will then have them taken every ten minutes after the first set. Of course, those vitals would be blood pressure, heart rate, respirations, lung sounds, temperature, and oxygen saturation. Checking their blood glucose is always a good idea because perhaps the person is hypoglycemic, and that's why they had a medical emergency.

THE CONVERSATION

How should that telephone conversation go with your EMS dispatcher? I have provided the following as an example for giving lifesaving information. Offering your information, as outlined below, will help move things along accurately and swiftly.

> I have an 83-year-old male who is conscious and breathing, complaining of chest pains with a history. I have a high index of suspicion for an MI.
>
> I have a 64-year-old female who is unconscious and apneic with no DNR in place. CPR is in progress.
>
> I have a 72-year-old male who is conscious with difficulty breathing. O_2 sats are 86% on room air, BP 84 over 60, with a heart rate of 130. We are in the process of administering supplemental O_2 via nasal cannula. (The 9-1-1 operator might want to keep you on the phone for the effectiveness of the nasal cannula.)

> I have an 89-year-old male who is conscious and breathing with a traumatic injury fall—high index of suspicion for pelvic fracture. Ten out of ten pelvic pain, right leg is longer than the left. Currently pulling a set of baseline vitals. (Again, because a pelvic fracture could be life-threatening, they might keep you on the telephone.)

Be sure that there is an escort from the door to the patient. Be sure gurneys, walkers, and residents are out of the way before EMS arrives. It should not be EMS personnel who clears your hallways. Moving your equipment or residents should be done by someone from your staff. The responding EMS personnel will significantly appreciate you for this assistance. Remember, it is an emergency! The goal is to get to the patient as quickly and efficiently as possible without causing additional incidents.

IF THE UNTHINKABLE HAPPENS

It is very distressing to me that I have to touch on this particular topic. It is tragic today that active shooter situations or other violence or hazards can happen in a place with such vulnerable people. But it can, and it does. Again, always follow the protocol and procedures of your particular Care Center.

As someone with tactical training as an EMT, our protocols changed to that we now go in with law enforcement during active shooter situations. What has been found is the sooner a medic can get to an individual and stop the bleeding, the better the outcome. Time is of the essence.

If you are unfortunate enough to have to endure any mass casualty at your center, remember that if someone isn't breathing when you're going through the sea of people who might be down, sometimes repositioning their head can open that airway but look for and stop bleeding as soon as possible. A blood pressure cuff also makes for an adequate tourniquet if you must.

Though it might sound morbid, I suggest everyone on staff carries a tourniquet. It just might save the life of your staff member, a resident, or even yourself. Ensure that everyone understands how to use them properly. Keep calm. Keep the victim or victims as calm as possible. And do your best to calm the walking wounded as well.

DNR?

When your residents are in stressful situations, some can begin to hyperventilate. They might pant because of personal stresses, or they're just frightened because of their medical condition. There is a difference between needing *Albuterol* because of asthma and hyperventilating as an emotional response. In these situations, there is something I will do with patients and even with my residents at the time.

When a resident or patient is hyperventilating, I will crouch before them and tell them to follow my breathing pattern. I will then breathe two breaths at their rate and then slow down. Doing this, they will breathe with me, and many will stop hyperventilation. This technique works most successfully on individuals at the beginning of that panicked breathing pattern.

Once at the Care Center, I was helping a resident with her breathing and overheard two nurses saying, "I don't know why she's bothering because that resident has a DNR order." In my mind, I thought, *Excuse me?* A DNR is not in play in this situation. *DNR* means *Do Not Resuscitate!* My resident was very much breathing. In fact, way too much! We don't give up simply because a resident has a DNR order. We work even harder for interventions before they get to that point of needing resuscitation because when they're gone, and we can't bring them back, they're gone!

NOTIFYING FAMILY MEMBERS

When a traumatic injury or illness causes you to send your resident to the emergency room, be sure to have all of the information at hand. Often, I saw leadership put CNAs in charge of making that call to the POA or family member who weren't very comfortable doing it. Some CNAs would unnecessarily panic the family member they called.

If you make that call, be as calm as possible when talking to family members. If they are frantic and upset with you because of the fall or medical condition, allow them to vent. As I will address later, people want to be heard. Stay calm and do not anger or panic them further. Be sure to have information regarding the hospital where their loved one will be sent or other information at hand. Your quick and accurate answers increases their confidence in you, the caregiver.

If the POA or family member is angry or frustrated, allow them to vent without trying to protect yourself from some supposed liability you might fear. You can say things like, "I understand you're upset, but your loved one is on the way to the hospital, and I am sure you will want to be there when they arrive. Please drive safely. They are in excellent hands." More on this in a later chapter.

Throughout this first segment, I hope you learned practical solutions for those training frustrations and glitches many Care Centers tend to experience that can cause individuals in the nursing staff to feel less confident and competent in their position. My hope is always to build confidence and help hone skills so that you can promote the longevity of the great staff you have working within your facility. All of this, of course, always leads to an increase in quality care which, again, I believe, is the goal for us all.

QUESTIONS FOR THOUGHT

1) How is the relationship with your EMS provider?
2) What areas of understanding were more significant for you as you reflected on the importance of giving the most accurate picture possible to the EMS dispatcher?
3) How do you help your staff deal with the difficulty of seeing a traumatic injury when they aren't accustomed to being exposed to such injuries?
4) How do you handle the heated conversations of family members who blame your center for the injury?
5) What is the importance of all staff members having a tourniquet? Will you ensure all your employees have one and train them on its use?

SECTION TWO

A POA Perspective And Bullying Prevention

4. Insight from a POA

Throughout the following three chapters of this book, I will draw not only from my experience in nursing but also from my ten years as the Power of Attorney (POA) for a loved one in a skilled nursing facility. I will also address the issue of bullying among residents. It can seem shocking for it to be necessary to speak to such a topic since we don't usually associate bullying with older adults. But for various reasons, it does happen.

Your residents' POA and family members can and should be your allies. In this three-chapter section, I address the Care Center's relationship with the POA or family member, including how that relationship can be helpful with bullying among residents. I hope you will gain better relationships with the POA or family members, and your residents will have better relationships with each other. The goal is that this information and training should lead to a happier, more thriving, and safer environment for everyone.

MEET CLARENCE

Perhaps it would be helpful to introduce you to Clarence Nagel, whom I met in 1994. I had conducted a training on another topic, and a reporter was among my attendees from a newspaper covering Southwest Washington and the Portland, Oregon area. Clarence had read her very kind article and wrote me a lovely letter. He also mentioned that he was a World War II Veteran who was very independent. I sent him a letter back thanking him for his encouragement. A day later, I had two letters in my mailbox. Shortly after that, I had three letters. And the letters kept coming! Since I lived in Southwest Washington, I knew I just had to meet him.

Clarence was eighty-eight years old and lived alone in the most humble circumstances. His entire apartment must have been only about five-hundred square feet in a not-so-safe neighborhood in Portland, Oregon. Developing this friendship, I would visit Clarence several times a month, take him to lunch, and check on him. My husband, Jeff, and I often enjoyed having him over to dinner as he became part of our family.

Once we had moved to our home in the *Hood-in-the-Wood* on the outskirts of Mount St. Helens Volcanic National Park, Jeff and I would often invite Clarence to move in with us understanding his humble circumstances and that the only financial help he got was through the Veterans Administration and a small amount through Social Security. He would roundly refuse, telling us that he was an old bachelor set in his ways. Though he often would share with me how he should have married "that widow woman," but lamented that her sons didn't like him. I could see there was a lot of regret with that missed opportunity.

However, in 1998 Clarence showed definite signs of decline. I would get phone calls from him asking for help financially which he had never done before. He would tell me he was confused with his checkbook and might have been overdrawn. Of course, we would help him like any family member, but something else became more evident. Jeff and I noticed that his short-term memory was going. He began to display confusion, and the dreaded confabulation, which took a bit to figure out. While pregnant with my son, I traveled and spoke during November of that same year and couldn't get to Portland to see him.

When my husband and I visited Clarnece to take him out for dinner during the Christmas rush, we were shocked at what we saw. He weighed about ninety pounds. It was obvious that we were witnessing a *failure-to-thrive* situation. Without even talking to each other, we looked at Clarence and said, "Great news, Clarence, you're going to be living with us from now on." He made no argument, realizing that it was the best for him.

Shortly after Clarence moved in with my husband, our six-year-old daughter, and me, I became his POA. The first thing I did for him was to connect him to every advantage he could get as a Veteran. He finally received new glasses and dentures and was seen by a Geriatric Specialist. We were able to increase his weight a little, but after a few syncope episodes, we were told he needed 24-hour nursing care.

There are some significant advantages to living in the woods. But as there are pros and cons with any living situation, we found it nearly impossible to find someone with appropriate medical and caregiving experience to come *all the way out* to our home. After other concerns, placing him in a Care Center was highly suggested.

Moving our loved one to a Care Center was one of the most difficult decisions Jeff and I have ever made. We understood the necessity for Clarence's health, but we could not shake the feeling that perhaps we had failed him somehow because we couldn't take care of him in our home any longer. While it wasn't an easy decision, we understood it was best for his greater good.

We found an appropriate Care Center that was suggested to us by a friend. Word of mouth is essential. Once there, his doctor recommended Clarence take a low-dose medication prescribed for depression, but it also worked to increase his appetite and would be temporary. The only medication

Clarence had ever taken was Tylenol. I gave a thumbs-up to this decision, and it began to work its magic.

One day I received a phone call from the Care Center that Clarence was having stomach pains. Distressed, I headed down immediately to talk with him since they couldn't find anything wrong. And then it hit me! I lifted his shirt and saw that Clarence had difficulty buttoning his pants. They would squeeze his newly widened waistline when he did. The issue wouldn't be resolved with additional medication but with an enjoyable shopping trip.

Clarence became very involved in the Care Center and relished every activity. I visited Clarence often, several times a week. In 2008 I received the phone call that Clarence had suffered a fall. They believed he was okay, but their protocol was to transport him to the hospital whenever their residents fell. Immediately I went to the hospital, and there was my Clarence in the emergency room with his hands behind his head, fingers interlocked, his legs outstretched on the gurney with his feet crossed in as casual and comfortable a pose as you could imagine. He greeted me with a huge smile, and I was relieved. I said, "Clarence, are you ready to go home?"

Clarence seemed a little confused about why he would be there in the first place and said, "Well, yeah, sure!" When one of the younger nursing staff members grabbed his arm, I could see when she pulled him up into a sitting position from being reclined that he began to grimace. I could tell while the fall didn't hurt Clarence, pulling him up the way she did caused something to go amiss.

When we returned to the Care Center, I told them I believed he hurt his side when they lifted him from the gurney. A few minutes later, a Physical Therapist came to his room asking him if he wanted physical therapy. Of course, having been very tired from his long day, he refused. The offer was never made again.

Clarence remained in bed, finally refusing all food and fluids. On July 2nd, 2008, I did manage to coax him out of his room and onto the patio to celebrate his 102nd birthday, and he even stayed long enough to take one bite of his cake. However, Clarence had given up, and on July 6th, 2008, Clarence Nagel went home to his eternal reward.

LESSONS LEARNED

I would say the Care Center did an excellent job with Clarence. However, there are some concerns I will pass on to you since they might be helpful. After Clarence had passed, I noticed that he had been placed on a powerful antipsychotic medication. I had no idea this had happened, as I was never informed. When I asked who approved putting him on such a medication when he had only been on a depression medication temporarily and remained on just Tylenol, a Charge Nurse (who was pretty new to that Care Center, who didn't know him, and didn't know me) was proud to say she had made that decision.

I felt the nurse's decision to place Clarence on a powerful antipsychotic medication was too much for somebody who had only taken a nightly Tylenol. I then asked her the reasoning for putting Clarence on such a medication. She said it was because he was displaying obsessive-compulsive behaviors. Her suggestion that he had any obsessive-compulsive disorder was indeed a surprise to me. Clarence was a great man of faith and had a lot of peace. I asked, "Clarence was an obsessive-compulsive?"

She said, "Yes. I believe he displayed the behaviors."

I asked, "Well, what did you observe about Clarence that made you think this?"

She answered, "Because he kept rubbing his legs and arms, and I asked him if he was cold, and he said he wasn't."

I asked, "Did it look like this?" and then vigorously rubbed my thighs. I said, "And did you notice Clarence did this too?" I started vigorously rubbing each of my arms, just as Clarence would.

She confidently replied, "Yes, yes, that's it!" I then realized she asked him the wrong question. Instead of asking if he was cold, she should have asked Clarence *why* he did that.

Clarence's response to that behavior would have been what he answered me when I once asked. He'd say, "I'm just sitting here not doing anything, so I rub my legs and arms to help keep the blood circulation going."

To give you a little insight into Clarence's mindset, he often said confidently, "I can run just as fast as I ever could, but why should I?" That should tell you a lot about him. Clarence saw himself as capable as he ever was. He did not see himself as a man in decline. Quite the opposite! He had no mental or emotional disorders—just joy, peace, faith, and gratitude.

However, Clarence was a health nut! He was very much into natural methods of healing yourself and believed that rubbing his legs and arms vigorously when just relaxing was a form of exercise for him. Clarence did not need to be on any anti-psych med, let alone a strong one that could make him lightheaded and dizzy and cause him to fall. We learned from previous chapters that asking the right questions is vitally important. That being said, I believe the staff at his Care Center extended Clarence's life by ten years. I don't have any severe complaints about his Care Center and the mostly marvelous team who worked there at that time.

TAP YOUR RESOURCES

If I had been asked by particular members of the staff at his Care Center, I would have given them an awful lot of insight into Clarence. Remember that the family member or POA can and should be your ally. I know we have conversations at the beginning when a resident first moves into the Care Center to help gain insight. The staff can learn about hobbies and past careers but must also know about triggers.

When I worked at the Care Center, I made it a point to find out which individuals were Veterans, so I could always honor them as such. Our Vietnam Veterans, who received a horrible homecoming, when honored, greatly appreciate it, and the number of surviving Korean War and World War II veterans is dwindling. I would have my son, who was in the Young Marine Youth Program for children ages eight to eighteen and other Young Marines, conduct Flag Folding Ceremonies during Veterans and Memorial Days. Once, a couple of the Young Marines couldn't make it, and at the last minute, my son, who held a high rank in the program, recruited a couple of residents who were World War II veterans to participate. It was an extraordinary moment for them and everyone in the room.

SHARE IT!

The necessary thing to note is that after gaining insight and information regarding your resident, whether from a POA, family member, or the client themselves, that information cannot simply be placed into a file where it can be forgotten. Be sure to pass that information on to caregivers. Remember, new caregivers will need that information as well. Having insight into your residents, such as past occupation, military service, unique hobbies, and triggers, will help nursing staff to have more compassion for and success with the individuals they serve since they have a greater understanding of them.

BE OBSERVANT

One afternoon I came to work on the Assisted Living side as a Med Tech and was told we had just gotten a new resident who wasn't cooperating well when taking her breathing treatments or other medications. Sally had been difficult for the nursing staff since she arrived a few days before. Understanding that this was a new resident who wasn't happy and probably wanted to communicate who was really in charge when I walked into her room, I began looking for something that I could use to strike up a conversation. What did I notice? A picture hung on the wall of a much younger version of the woman standing before me, holding a large trophy she had gotten from a bowling competition. I looked at the picture and said, "Oh my goodness, is that you?"

Though pretty small, Sally appeared to gain an inch in height right before my eyes as she proudly looked at the picture of herself. Then looking over at me, she said, "Yes, it is."

I said, "Wow, that's amazing!" The timing was perfect because it just so happened my husband's company was going to have their Christmas party at a bowling alley. I mentioned this to her and explained that I always have some challenges with turning my wrist after a while of bowling. I asked her if she had any suggestions since I didn't want to embarrass myself before my husband and his coworkers. She was very eager to share her insights with me.

I then said to Sally, "Oh, I'm so sorry. Here I am, enjoying our chat, and I completely forgot I have to give you your treatments and medications. I'm so sorry. Let me grab them for you." By apologizing, I reminded Sally that I was well aware of the fact that *I* worked for *her*. It was a subtle way of letting her know I knew who the client was and that I was to serve her. She appreciated the respect.

What was Sally's response to my apology? She said, "No problem!" and took her medication without incident. I never had any challenges with Sally. All it took was a couple of minutes and a little common ground. But it also took knowing something about the individual I would serve to build that bridge of trust and respect.

Those two elements, trust, and respect, are crucial in the relationship between the family, caregivers, and residents. I recognized something in Clarence that I also realized in my residents years later as a caregiver. If a resident I served felt their needs were not respected, they would stop communicating their needs if they were treated as an annoyance, inconvenience, or burden. Their silence has definite hazards because if there are changes in their medical condition, they will not feel comfortable and will not be candid enough to express what those are. You want your residents to talk to you. If they only wish to speak with their family members concerning those changes, hopefully, their POA or family member feels comfortable enough to pass that information on to you.

UNDERMINING TRUST

Sometimes trust can be unwittingly undermined in the relationship with a resident's POA or family member. Trust is pivotal for positive relationships, especially when the nursing staff is tasked with the care and medical treatment of their loved ones.

I will never forget one Charge Nurse who, for whatever reason, was unhappy about having Clarence in her care. She always talked about how it would be more appropriate for him to be in an Alzheimer's unit. Knowing Clarence, I realized this would be utterly inappropriate for him. If you took a moment, he was easy to redirect and, otherwise, very friendly and reasonable. Whenever she was on duty, that particular Charge Nurse would call and dramatically say, "We have big problems with Clarence!" I always wondered how they could have *big problems* with him.

The first few times this nurse called me, I would immediately hop in my car and take the hour drive as fast as possible to get to the Care Center, only to find him entirely at peace. She would then say, "Well, he's okay now, but he was very agitated, wanted to go for a walk, and didn't want to wait." After a while, anytime I received a phone call from her, I would get off the phone and call one of the other caregivers. They would usually say, "Clarence is fine. He wanted to go out for a walk, and we asked him if he could wait about ten minutes until one of us finished giving a treatment or shower, and then we'd be glad to take him. He waited the ten minutes, and we walked together. There was no problem."

The POA or family member knows who they can trust and who they can't. They know who will tell them straight-up what's going on and those who will hedge. They also learn from whom they can get information. I will go into detail on that in a later chapter.

CONNECTING

The activities director at the Care Center where Clarence lived immediately noticed he was a tinkerer. He would tinker with anything! His skilled nursing facility discovered this by making the mistake of putting someone in his room with a machine that would periodically beep. For Clarence, that beep meant something was wrong with the device, and he would have to fix it. I don't think it's necessary to tell you that they stopped putting anyone in with Clarence who required anything with an alarm. Since the activities director recognized this about Clarence, she gave him a little oil can. He would then proceed to oil door hinges and, upon request, wheelchairs. It gave him a purpose. She observed him and recognized a need other than medical in my Clarence. And I think he so enjoyed quieting those squeaky places, knowing he had an impact to help make things run more smoothly. As his POA, I cannot express how much it meant that she was observant and did something to fulfill this need within him—that moment of realization built trust so I could sleep at night, knowing that he was in good care.

By giving a little oil can to Clarence, the activities director treated him as an individual and saw him as an individual. He was not reduced to a room number. His needs were met. When caregivers ask, "Would you prefer this done this way or that way?" As often as possible, the resident feels empowered by showing them they are respected as individuals. This respect offers security to the family members or POA in letting them know that you are genuinely concerned about meeting the needs of their loved one.

VALIDATE

There was something I found very beneficial to me when I was in corporate sales and customer service. I also share it with people in my communication and presentation training when dealing with someone who might be angry during a question-and-answer session. When your POA or family member is upset or frustrated, stop looking for ways to shut down the conversation or change the subject because, again, you're terrified of regulation and liability. So often, I saw nursing staff or leadership within a Care Center immediately defend themselves or the center if there was a negative situation. However, even if the family member or power of attorney is wrong, you can still validate. Validating does not mean that you agree with them or that their position is correct. It simply diffuses the situation and allows the family member to feel heard. Sometimes that's all people want.

You can use statements like, "I can see you're upset." Or, "I can see this is very important to you." Or "I understand your concern." I regularly change the word *problem* to *concern*. It lightens up the situation but also tells those who are frustrated or angry that I am compassionate enough to listen to what they have to say. It also leaves them more open to the solution I offer. When you automatically go into defense mode, voices become louder and angrier because the other individual will feel as if you are not hearing them.

WHEN FAMILY MEMBERS CAN'T SEE

Certain situations can place the nursing staff against the POA or family member, creating an antagonistic relationship. I would see this as a First Responder, and I would have to have another responder remove specific individuals from the room because things would become heated during my attempts to assess my patient.

Sometimes it is difficult for family members to see their mother or father as frail and needing assistance. Many of them can go into denial regarding their parent or grandparents' actual condition. Perhaps their loved one was a pillar in the community, did a great deal for their family, and was the one everyone else relied upon. Seeing their parents getting older means they are, too. For some adult children of those you serve, that can be hard to grasp. It can also be traumatic for some adult children to realize their parent is now in the twilight of their life.

Frustrations can build, especially during an assessment. It can cause friction between the caregiver, other staff, and the POA or family member. They might become frustrated because they feel like you refuse to see their loved one as capable as they do. In reality, you see them in an accurate light in their frailty. You understand specific disease processes and what happens in aging.

Sometimes a family member can become very angry with their loved one. You might ask the resident, or potential resident, a question and receive an expression of confusion or an attempt to try to remember something from the past. The family member could become very frustrated with their aging parent and say, “Come on, Mom, you know the answer.” They will then look at you and angrily state, “She knows this. I don't know why she's not telling you.” However, the fact is mom probably just can't remember. The family member can become angry and frustrated with the potential caregiver for not posing the question correctly, or they are dismayed that their loved one is refusing to answer or answer accurately!

In an attempt to diffuse what could be a very heated situation, I usually say, “Tell me about Mom.” They might then tell me how she would bake cakes for everybody's birthday or create blankets for individuals in the community who suffered from illness. Perhaps they would say she would help people in the neighborhood with their gardens. Or maybe she taught at the local school. To which I then ask, “What year was that?” I always want them to be specific. If I ask, “How long ago was that?” They'll state that it was just a few years ago. However, I want them to give me a specific year. More often than not, it was more than 15 or 20 years ago.

I then slowly and softly say, "Wow, that long ago? Do you realize that's almost 20 years ago?" As they step back and think, I slowly and methodically state, "Well, how do you see Mom now?" Suddenly they take another look at their Mom and see her in a whole new light. As I recognize their expression change and they come to this painful reality, lightening things up, I remind them that this is a new season for Mom. I will then state, "It sounds like she has served everybody else. Now it is time for us to have the honor and privilege of caring for her, allowing her to put her feet up and feel spoiled."

Please be sensitive in these situations. It is so easy to say it like it is so you can move on to other things. But remember, the one hurting the most isn't always your resident.

QUESTIONS FOR THOUGHT

1) Is the POA or family member your ally? Take a moment and think about this unique relationship.
2) What has worked for you in building bridges to make this relationship better? Take those skills and pass them on to your caregivers.
3) What has worked for your caregivers? Many of them have tremendous insight, as I had. All someone had to do was ask!
4) What has not worked in your relationship with the POA or family member, and why?
5) What frustrations are your staff facing in the relationship with the POA or family member? Perhaps you can use this training to help make that relationship better.

5. Addressing the Resident Bully

As I began imparting my *LPNequip.org* training across the United States for Health Care Association conferences or conventions, I had repeated requests from numerous attendees to address one specific topic. It remains surprising to me that it would be necessary to address this since we all hope that by the time we are in the later stages of life, we will mature to the point where training for it would not be necessary. However, you don't have to work at a Care Center for long until you realize that bullying among residents needs to be *tackled*.

I think the first key to understanding is defining what the word *bullying* means since there are vital elements in the definition that you must be aware of when addressing this topic. Before you can solve a challenge, you first have to define it accurately. As with any challenge, knowing the problem is essential to overcoming it. As I looked into the various definitions, I aimed to make the definition easy to remember. Therefore, I consolidated it into one sentence. Here is what I came up with:

> *Bullying is intentional, repetitive, aggressive behavior involving an imbalance of power by another individual with the need to control.*

The above is what bullying is in a nutshell. The two biggest takeaways from that definition are an *imbalance of power* and *the need to control*.

Unfortunately, no reliable statistics show how many people are on the victim end of bullying because there is a lot of fear among those who might want to report it. There is also a lot of shame that goes along with being bullied. Nobody wants to be seen as a victim. Let alone to be one! Folks can feel embarrassed at admitting that someone has that type of power or control over them. Bullying can happen to anyone. It can happen regardless of how old a person is or their gender. It doesn't matter the amount of melanin in someone's skin or from what socioeconomic background they hail. Anyone can be the target of a bully.

TACTICS

Now that we have defined it, we can examine the particulars of bullying. It is valuable to understand the various tactics employed by a bully. Knowing this information will help you to realize the distinction between bullying or if it's just annoying behavior. To liven things up a bit, because lists can be very dull, I've assigned a name to each explanation of the type of bullying the named individual would employ. Now, just because there is one name for each bully tactic in my list, some residents in your Care Center might use multiple tactics below. You might have one resident who bites, gossips, and controls. So be aware of that as you review what I've compiled.

You might wonder how or why I can easily outline these characteristics. Until a significant worldview change over thirty years ago, I was the victim of several bullies. Besides, it is not hard to spot the techniques and behavior because human nature is human nature, as you will see. Now, let's take a look!

1. Yolanda Yeller becomes loud or will yell at her victim in public to instill fear in them and to alert others that, *This could be you*. When people hear someone yelling in a public setting, they generally aren't looking at the person yelling.

They want to know who's the target. Onlookers then wonder what that individual did to make Yolanda so upset. Many people will keep silent or coddle the bully to avoid being the focus of Yolanda's publicly loud and obnoxious tantrums.

2. Katie Critic will engage in name-calling and taunt her victim, perhaps teasing them. She can be very sarcastic as she criticizes them about anything that will give them the highest sense of shame or discomfort.

3. Freddy Fake-Friendly might draw people in to learn personal information. Then Freddy will backstab and gossip to the point of inventing stories to spread hurtful rumors. Your staff often fears this resident because Freddy has no problem ruining another person's reputation. Your team will do anything to get on the good side of Freddy so as not to become his target.

4. Penny Pincher becomes physical with her victims. She might push them or shove them. She might deliberately fall up against or trip them. She might even bite and, of course, pinch! This physical harm is not something that Care Centers can tolerate.

5. Oliver Opportunist waits for his victim to be at their most vulnerable. Then he will pounce! Perhaps he noticed another resident returning from their doctor's appointment and might have received bad news. Maybe they've just returned from an outing and are exhausted, or Oliver notices his victim is sad after a particular visitor leaves. It doesn't matter. Oliver will seize every opportunity to bully. There is genuine cruelty in this type of bullying.

6. Paul Pilfer subtly removes or damages the property of his victims. Usually, he is shocked that someone would find their things in his possession or hidden in his room. Paul employs excellent acting skills when found out.

7. Mini Mime can display rude or mean gestures and facial expressions. She will mimic someone she doesn't like to bring ridicule to that person causing others to laugh at her victim. Her victim will then attempt to change their behavior or mode of dress or character to stop the laughter at their expense. Mini can prompt a sense of paranoia in her victims.

8. Connie Control is someone I think we have all seen at our workplace. She will exclude others from her social click. Connie gains followers only because they are terrified of being on the outs from the cool crowd. If you're going to have an idea, it better coincide with Connie, or you will be booted publicly from her inner circle. If Connie isn't going to associate with her victim, you better not either!

9. Pat Passion slowly but surely and with little subtly invades another person's space. Pat will be shocked if you call him out and brush off his unwanted sexual advances as if it's all in your head! It's not. He's doing it to pursue his passions or simply to make his victim feel uncomfortable.

10. Gary Gaslighter replaces fact with fiction by creating flaws in his victim that never existed. This behavior results in a host of insecurities the victim feels. For example, they might tell their victim they are talking *way too loud*. The victim then lowers their voice so even others cannot hear them. Since some people keep asking the victim to speak louder, and Gary is telling them to hush up, the victim does just that. Withdraws and stops talking to others.

I know of a victim whose gaslighting family member will preface her *helpful correction* by first saying, "There is something you do, and it's a very bad thing that you do." When the gaslighter has her victim's full attention, she points out something completely benign that cannot possibly be changed. It makes the victim feel paranoid about everything the bully points out. Not nice.

11. Mary Martyr is very good at twisting things and turning the tables to make the victim seem like the perpetrator, thus making herself out to be the victim! Mary can sit in front of you with a sympathetic voice and say, "Please don't say anything, but I don't know why Jodie would do such a thing, but this is what she did..." all the while playing the innocent. Mary will pin people against the victim. Since she prefaced what she said with, "Please don't say anything," folks feel uncomfortable going to the victim to explain why they no longer talk to them. Don't buy into it if someone uses this preface to draw you into drama and use you to further Mary's bullying tactic!

12. Jesse Jester can make rude, demeaning, and hurtful jokes at his victim's expense. When the victim expresses hurt or offense, Jesse quickly says, "I'm just kidding. Can't you take a joke?" Unfortunately, the damage is done, the joke has been made, the nickname has been heard, or the slur is repeated by others. While the victim might attempt to look as if they have a sense of humor about it, they are hurting from the sting of Jesse's words and the others who might pile on.

THE MAKING OF A BULLY

There is something else to consider before we can address solutions to bullying among residents in our next chapter. I believe it is essential to understand what might contribute to a resident in your Care Center becoming a bully. There are several factors to keep in mind.

As individuals age, they often isolate themselves from others. Various events or circumstances can cause people to do this. It could be hearing loss, loss of sight, or depression over losing many loved ones over the years, which can result in palpable loneliness. The more they pull back and the longer they are isolated from people, the harder it can be for them to adjust to constantly being around others. This separation could create inner anger and decrease social skills, which could be expressed through bullying.

Unfortunately, you could also have a Care Center resident who lacks empathy. For that bully, it just might be a foreign language to them that someone might be hurt by something they've said or done. Something within them is fractured, causing them to lack empathy and compassion for others outside of themselves.

Another possibility is that they might have unresolved anger issues. Sometimes life can kick us hard. But when you take a step back and think about your residents for a moment, some people have spent their lives building a home, looking forward to retirement years, only to find out that the older they become, what they face is a loss of independence, loss of friends and loved ones, unfinished business with those who have passed on or people who refuse to take the time to make amends for past hurts. These issues and events seem to magnify in the older years, especially when these individuals have time to brood over them. The various events or issues your predisposed bully is brooding over are rotten ingredients that can add to a recipe for rotten behaviors.

THE MAKING OF A VICTIM

Since I have addressed the tactics of a bully and what could potentially make someone engage in that behavior, it is time to consider the victim. Are there characteristics that make it easier for someone to be a target? There sure are.

Bullies prefer to look for someone who appears weak. The bully doesn't usually pick on people they think might bully back. They would look for someone who looks vulnerable, as with *Oliver Opportunist*. The weak and the vulnerable appear to the bully as if their victim would never have the strength to admit that they were on the receiving end of their tactics.

When we think of what could make someone a victim of bullying, of course, we have to consider that anyone who comes into the Care Center as a new resident could appear to be a threat to individuals like *Connie Control*. Therefore they can become an instant target until they learn their place will not be at the *cool kid's* table until they have earned it through compliance with the bully.

CLARA vs. CLARENCE

Something else can make a resident the target of a bully. The potential victim might look like or remind the bully of someone from their past. When Clarence was in the care facility, he always seemed to be paired up with a woman named Clara. Clara had been a nurse, so she would drive the nursing staff crazy by looking at the conditions of the other residents and then would alert the nurses at the nurse's station as if they weren't on their job. Everyone at his Care Center thought Clara and Clarence were so cute together. They would pair them up at events and during Christmas as Ma and Pa Santa.

However, in observing Clara and Clarence together, while many on the staff thought it was adorable, I noticed they argued an awful lot. They did not seem as if they were as happy as the staff members were with the arrangement. There always seemed to be a lot of friction between them.

One day Clara became angry and impatient with Clarnece and smacked him on his arm. However, Clarence wasn't having any of that and returned the favor. The relationship was cute to the staff no longer. At that juncture, I thought I'd chat with Clara to understand a bit of the *why* behind what I witnessed. As it turned out, to my horror, Clarence reminded Clara of her abusive ex-husband simply because of his appearance! The information that Clarence was a *trigger* for Clara would have been vital for deciding if they should be paired for anything at any time.

IMPACT ON STAFF

While some might think that someone in their eighties having the zeal and strength to bully others might be small and perhaps somewhat humorous, bullying among residents can negatively affect the people who work for your Care Center. That impact is felt particularly hard by your nursing staff. It might be emotionally difficult for some of your staff members to witness. If they, too, have been or quite possibly are the victim of a bully in their personal lives, seeing bullying among your residents could trigger them. Because they are a victim themselves or have been in the past, they might not feel strong enough to speak up and then can feel tremendous guilt for not intervening.

Some individuals in your employ might not get involved because they are afraid they will become the target of that powerful personality. Because they need their position at your Care Center to feed their family, their fear of that resident might cause them to hold back on reporting it, not wanting to get involved.

Bullying among residents creates terrible instability within a Care Center. It makes everyone uncomfortable. Some become irritated with the bully, while others fear them. Staff members can also feel uncomfortably embarrassed as they witness the victim squirm yet feel helpless to do or say anything. People don't like to feel uncomfortable. This discomfort with the bully or victim's presence is why other residents might ask who will attend a particular outing. If they see the names of the victim and the bully on the list, they just might pass on the opportunity because they don't feel like experiencing that dynamic.

SIGNS AND SYMPTOMS

What should we look out for when it comes to bullying? The victim might refuse to join other residents for trips involving a bus ride. They might constantly request a room tray and do anything to avoid entering the dining room. Sometimes you can tell who is the bully or victim simply by looking at the eye contact. The bully will look straight at that victim, whereas the victim will look anywhere else but at the bully. As soon as the bully arrives in the dining room, the victim might lower their gaze or will suddenly fidget with something to avoid eye contact. If there are gatherings where the bully and victim might be in the same room, the victim will usually withdraw from the events and anything else that would follow.

Bullying affects the victim's health because it elevates their anxiety level, which can be seen when they are around particular residents. You will also notice your resident feeling depressed because they feel socially isolated. Bullying can also exacerbate the disease process because of the stress of being the victim.

Finally, you will probably hear the victim express their desire to move to another facility or say they want to *go home*. Due to fear or embarrassment, your resident might not articulate the reason for their pleas to leave your facility. Again, no one wants to admit that they are a bullying victim.

Heartbreaking, I know, but now that I have laid out some of the elements to be aware of regarding residents bullying each other in this chapter, I hope to offer some help regarding what you can do about it in the next.

QUESTIONS FOR THOUGHT

1. What is the definition of bullying, as I have explained in this chapter?
2. When you consider your Care Center, are there residents you know who employ some of the same tactics as the fictitious individuals I have outlined?
3. Have family members shared information with you regarding their loved one being the victim of a resident bully?
4. Have you seen any adverse effects of resident bullying on your staff members?
5. Do you see elements for the making of a bully in any resident you currently serve? Have you taken steps to help that individual?

6. Help for Bullies and Victims

With a step back, a deep breath, and a clear picture, it is time to move forward and address solutions regarding the resident bully. I hope to offer practical answers for the victims and allow you to see where you can enlist and involve the POA or family member to help make working and living conditions at your Care Center better for all!

DON'T HESITATE

If you have a hint that bullying is happening in your Care Center, you have to address it immediately. As the saying goes, *if you see something, say something*, and if warranted, do file an incident report. Ignoring the bullying dynamic can enable the bullying and allow it to continue. I suggest you address it with staff and then with your residents using general terms with no specific names.

If it continues once you've addressed it as a group, address it one-on-one with the individuals involved. It is essential to determine what prompted the bullying situation. Could it simply be a misunderstanding? Could one individual be a trigger for another? You will not know unless you investigate. If necessary, you might want to suggest professional counseling because of the emotional state some residents can be in when they enter your Care Center.

MUSICAL CHAIRS

In certain situations, especially with a *Connie Control*, I have noticed that bullies like to save seats for their favorite *yes*-peeps. They will regard a particular table in the dining room, which happens to have the best view of the courtyard, as their own. Don't allow this to happen. If at all possible, mix things up! Change the seating in your dining room and gathering areas like your foyer. For some Memory Care Centers, I understand this might be impossible. But try to mix it up a bit where it is possible. When you move the chairs around, you move the people around, and they might sit with individuals whom they don't usually talk to.

Another thing you can do would be to have a staff member escort each resident to a seat, perhaps have them seated with someone they don't usually sit with because they might never have had the chance to meet. With a staff member switching up the seating each night as they are escorted in, it is a great way to break down those walls and get people to talk with and meet others they might feel more comfortable with than a *Connie Control.*

PLAYING FAVORITES

In my time at the Care Center, and from comments I receive as I share my training, certain staff members, including those in leadership positions, will refuse to address the resident bully. Instead, they will go out of their way to coddle them. By indulging this mischief maker, they think they will not become a target for bullying. Don't kid yourself! Coddling or pampering a bully is a sign of weakness. They know you're doing it. But what you are also doing is giving them more power. If you are guilty of coddling a bully, it's time to own your role! Take responsibility, and don't let them take advantage of you, your staff, or your residents. You are not helping the victims in your Care Center. You are empowering the bully to continue to abuse others.

ENLISTING HELP

The powerful dynamic I address in this chapter is one where you will need the resident's POA or family member as an ally. If you suspect a bullying situation in your Care Center, enlist and encourage your resident's family members to communicate changes, signs (what they see in their loved one), or symptoms (what their loved one states they feel) regarding their condition, conversation, or behavior to the leadership in your Care Center. Also, let the family members know whether their loved one is the bully or the victim. They might be able to nip it in the bud pretty quickly because of their familial relationship.

Work with the POA or family member for a shared understanding and solution. Perhaps every so often, they can sit with their loved one when dining or with them where others gather to help the victim feel more comfortable and to let the bully know that their victim has an ally. Many times if the bully sees that there is an ally, they will be less apt to continue in their bad behavior. Yes, there is strength in numbers.

Family members who are frustrated if you lack the fortitude to do anything about their loved one being bullied in your Care Center might prompt them to take matters into their own hands. That is not a situation you want. Let the POA or family know you are on top of it. Even if they are unaware, letting them know before they realize the unfortunate dynamic will build their confidence in your suggestions and care. You will then gain a powerful ally.

POLICIES AND PROCEDURES

Because this is *supplemental* training and not a book with detailed regulations, policy particulars, or specific Assisted Living or long-term care procedures, I will refer you to the professionals in those areas. Thus, I will continue to suggest that your staff understands and follows your Care Center's policies and procedures. Be sure to instill in the residents, the family members or POA, and caregivers that you will enforce specific no-tolerance policies and procedures with clear expectations from everybody. Include boundaries that, if crossed, can result in definite consequences. If you state consequences, be sure to follow through. Your policies must encourage and make it more comfortable for victims and staff to report what they witness or experience.

Always have a process to resolve the situation. Perhaps counseling, or if necessary, mediation would be appropriate, but always be sure to outline consequences for those who continue to bully.

Review your policies and procedures with your staff often. Don't be afraid to update or adjust them as you develop a better game plan. Always ensure they are readily available and allow plenty of training and retraining for your staff members.

When you attend Health Care Association (HCA) events, remember to ask other attendees throughout your state how they address bullying at their Centers. These statewide events are vital for Care Center personnel to connect and learn—not just from the workshops or keynote addresses—but from each other.

Again, enforce your policies and procedures with your staff, residents, and their POA or family when necessary. Everyone needs to be on the same page regarding the challenge of bullying. Zero or spotty compliance will result in zero impact.

For a moment, think about what happens with children who are told, "If you don't behave, I'm going to take away that ice cream cone." When they continue to misbehave and realize they can finish their ice cream uninterrupted, that means to them there really aren't any consequences. They can continue with bold behavior because they know you won't do anything about it. Your action must be palpable. Your follow-through will give comfort not only to your victim, but it will let the other residents know that you will not tolerate bullying in your Care Center. Your Care Center is then viewed as a place of safety. Your residents, their family members, and your entire staff will realize the benefits of this.

HELP FOR VICTIMS

Always be sure victims know that they do have a voice. Let them know they can respectfully speak up and stand up for themselves. Let them know they can communicate such challenges with your staff and their family.

One way to alleviate new residents from being bullied is by having a mentor program. Perhaps you can have new residents come under the wing of a kind and trusted resident. We can all think of that *Betty Butterfly*, who loves meeting new people and is kind to everyone. Perhaps this would be the ideal individual to take that new person under her wing and introduce them to other residents in your Care Center. Maybe she can introduce them to individuals with common interests.

AVOID BEING A TARGET

There are several ways to avoid being a target of a bully. Some of these suggestions we can pass on to our residents. One is that we can simply ignore the tactics of the bully. Once the bully sees that their tactic doesn't work, it eliminates their power. Also, maintaining a sense of humor is very helpful. Making light of it and laughing it off also removes the power of the one trying to get under their skin.

Provocations can also be avoided. These are things that might trigger the bully into action. Or anyone, for that matter! For example, interrupting someone while still speaking can be frustrating to a resident who already takes a moment to gather their thoughts while explaining something. Of course, this can be a cultural thing as well!

I grew up in the metropolitan area of New York City, where cutting people off and interrupting them mid-sentence wasn't an offense. If I was finishing your sentence, it meant I was tracking with you in agreement. I finished what you had to say, not because I was in a hurry and you talked too slowly, but as a way of communicating, *I agree with you!* However, when I moved to California at twenty-one years old and did the same thing, the response I got was, "You talked right over me. You're not even listening to what I'm saying! You only want to say what you want to say!" Ouch! I encountered many misunderstandings and had to learn the hard way to hush my mouth until someone finished what they were saying. So some things could indeed be cultural.

We also find that everyone seems to have an opinion on everything. When residents forcefully share their views, they can turn people off, creating a bully-victim scenario. Perhaps a staff member can gingerly mention, "You know what, Mollie, Miss Susie isn't very interested in that type of thing, but Mr. Steven is. Perhaps you would like to share that information with him?"

While it is true that maintaining eye contact with the bully is also a good tactic as it conveys a sign of strength and confidence, sometimes it just takes a change in thinking when one considers what can be happening in the heart of the individual who bullies. When I take time to stand in their shoes and think about how it probably doesn't feel the best to be that type of person, it gives me more compassion for them. I couldn't imagine how sickening it would feel to be the one in the room who enjoys making other people's lives miserable. What a sad existence!

SUMMING IT UP!

I hope this segment of the last three chapters helped you better understand your resident's POA or family members and how they should be and can be your ally. I also hope you found the information helpful on how to *tackle* bullying among residents, with the desire, of course, that you would have successful relationships between residents, and the residents with staff, for a safer, healthier, and happier environment for all.

QUESTIONS FOR THOUGHT

1. What is your response if you discover bullying between residents at your Care Center? Was the POA or family member helpful in that situation? Why or why not?
2. When was the last time you discussed bullying among residents with your staff? Is it time to revisit this?
3. Have you been guilty of coddling a resident bully? If so, was it helpful?
4. Do you have a *Betty Butterfly* in your Care Center? Could she help to bring residents together?
5. Have you asked caregivers who have perhaps worked in other Care Centers how they dealt with bullying in the past? Find out what worked and what didn't work for them.

SECTION THREE

Building a Positive Work Environment: It Begins With Staff

7. Building Memories, Not Misery

Throughout the following three chapters, I want to address the fact that if you are a leader, you have the responsibility and the power to impact your work environment for good. I hope you will do what you can to make your Care Center the best it can be so everyone looks forward to walking through those front doors rather than rolling their eyes as they enter.

THE CULTURE OF MEAN

Approximately five years ago, when I first started the *LPNequip.org* training, an article came across my desk about a female Navy Corpsman who worked in the maternity ward of a Naval Hospital in Florida. This Navy Nurse and a few of her friends thought it would be funny to blast music and play with the newborns in their care as though they were toys. They held and bounced them around as if to give these fragile newly born babies the appearance that they were dancing as the nurse uploaded their cruelty onto a social media app. She believed her not-so-funny comedy video would only be available for twenty-four hours. Thus, in the Corpsman's mind, only her *friends* would see it and think it was fun and funny too. Thankfully, one of the nurse's *friends* did not get the joke and instead took screenshots and reported her. As her actions went viral, the result was the loss of her valued and enviable position and embarrassment for her and her family, who perhaps supported her in attaining her coveted position in that hospital.

When we think about all that young woman went through to attain her position, some of us might be scratching our heads and asking ourselves how it could happen. How could this Navy Corpsman be so irresponsible? Was stupidity her problem? Perhaps she was uneducated and not the sharpest scalpel in the box. However, let's consider what it took to attain her position in a Florida Naval hospital.

That woman in the article would have to have done reasonably well in high school to pass the Armed Services Vocational Aptitude Battery (ASVAB) to get into the military and qualify for her Military Occupational Specialty (MOS) to attain Navy Corpsman. She would then have to qualify and successfully complete Naval boot camp as a woman. She then must complete her MOS schooling to become a Naval Corpsman. After all that achievement, she was not attached to some Marine Unit in a foreign country with bugs as big as her head but got to work as a nurse in a maternity ward in her home country for a Naval Hospital in the beautiful state of Florida.

I lay all this before you to prove my point that having graduated high school successfully, passed the ASVAB successfully, graduated boot camp successfully, and graduated her MOS training successfully, her downfall obviously wasn't because she wasn't educated. As we take a step back, I have to believe that we are indeed living in a *culture of mean*. One perusal of social media, the Corpsman's video included, proves that with absolute certainty.

A LESSON FROM BOULDERS

Considering the workplace and your impact, you should first realize that a bad attitude can be like a boulder rushing downhill as it crushes everything in its path. Suppose you are a leader in your organization. In that case, you can crush the ambition level of your subordinates, you can crush a willingness to share ideas that could impact your Center for good, you can crush the spirits of individuals who are simply trying to make a living to support their family, and you can crush their spirit to the point where they say, "I've had enough." It's a rotten way to lose good people.

I have had the experience of this boulder rolling downhill in the Care Center where I once worked. As you can gather, I was always very conscientious about those in my care. One afternoon, as I was about to take my dinner break, I wanted to alert the Charge Nurse, who was working on the long-term care side, of some health challenges one of my residents was experiencing in case something went sideways while I was gone. I also wanted to pass off the keys to the cart so he had them. I was being responsible!

I walked through the double doors to the long-term care side of the facility and down the hallway toward where the Charge Nurse stood in front of a med cart. From behind me at the nurse's station, I heard the angry voice of my DON yell, "Judy Salisbury, what are you doing here?" Stunned that anyone would so rudely address me, I slowly turned around and looked at her like she had four heads. She said, "You shouldn't be here! You are supposed to be in Assisted Living. You need to get back over there right now!"

Other nurses were in the nurse's station, CNAs and a few residents with their family members were throughout the busy hallways. Everyone was looking on to watch for my reaction. If only there had been popcorn!

I then casually strolled over, put my hand in the pocket of my *Cat-in-the-Hat* themed scrub top, and grabbed the keys. With a monotone voice, I said to this woman I greatly respected, "I think I'm done here." With one finger, I then slid the keys across the counter of the nurse's station to her, looking her right in the eye as I calmly stated, "I need a break." I then left. Well, I had to. I had already clocked out for dinner!

After my break, I returned to my office in Assisted Living to ready the cart for the evening med pass. There, in my office, at the cart, was the Charge Nurse whom I was initially going to inform of my resident's condition and then hand him the keys. He was there to begin prepping for my evening med pass. He looked at me and said, "Oh, thank goodness you came back!"

I said, "Of course, I came back. I just went to dinner."

He said, "We all thought you quit!"

I chuckled, saying, "No, I didn't quit."

He handed me the keys and said, "It really wasn't you. You were fine. But you do know why that happened, don't you?"

With a grin, I said, "No, but you're going to fill me in, aren't you?"

He said, "Well, every time the Administrator has a bad day, she takes it out on the Nursing Director."

And there, of course, you have a boulder rolling downhill. I happened to have met it at the bottom of that hill at just the right time. I said, "That's very interesting. Thanks for the heads-up. I will remember that."

Everyone in the facility seemed to be working late that evening as they knew *Survey* was looming. Suddenly, I saw the DON begin to walk past my office door when she saw me, stopped short in her tracks, and came in. She said with a smile and almost a giggle, "Oh, you're back!"

I could see the relief on her face. I closed my cart, looked at her, and stated with a composed, serious tone, "Yes, I'm back. Of course, I am. But I'll tell you right now, don't ever do that to me again. You can talk to me calmly, without yelling. If you have a question or concern or believe I'm doing something incorrectly, and if you think you cannot maintain a calm voice, bring me into your office, and we'll discuss it. But don't ever do that to me in a public area again. I do not deserve that."

She humbly said, "No, you're right, you don't. I'm so sorry." She seemed sincerely regretful about it. We hugged it out and moved on.

However, that Administrator was in the back of my mind. A little while later, I caught a glimpse of her getting coffee in the empty dining room. The Administrator was a woman who could intimidate just about anybody, and she knew it. However, I think she was a bit intrigued by me. I think she knew I didn't need that job. (In the last segment of this book, I will explain why I decided to get my license and work in a Care Facility.)

I casually walked up to her, leaned toward her as she poured her coffee, and said as if I were telling her a secret, "Hey, I hear you're having a bad day?"

She shrugged and said, "Oh, I don't know."

I said, "Well, you know how to cure a bad day and bad attitude in one shot, don't you?"

She sarcastically said, "No, how?" she then sipped her coffee with an anticipatory look.

I said in the same hushed tone, "You go over to the long-term care side of this facility, into the room of the most frail and fragile resident, and ask yourself if you would rather trade your worst day for their best day. It's incredible how gratitude works wonders! Next time you want to grumble at somebody, try that." I then left her there with her coffee. I don't know if she ever took the prescription.

Changing the culture is a decision everyone needs to make. Creating a better environment for those around you is an absolute choice, and you have to ask yourself if you are willing to decide to impact for good those places where you step your foot. Is it possible to do that? Absolutely. Do the people you work with need that? You bet they do. People are getting hammered, it seems, from every angle, and if you can uplift them in some way and you have the opportunity and power to do so, then it is your obligation, your duty as a human being and leader, to do just that. Are you willing? If you are still reading this book, I would say your answer is a resounding *YES!*

YOU'RE STUCK WITH EACH OTHER

You will spend more time with the people you work with if you work full time than with family members in your household. Therefore, you can consider your workplace an extension of your family. But, ask yourself, *What kind of a dysfunctional family would I like us to be?* Because we are dealing with human beings who have flaws, make mistakes, have mood changes, and everything else that goes with being human, we are all dysfunctional in some ways. Therefore, do we want to be the miserable dysfunctional family or the motivated and fun dysfunctional family? I don't know about you, but I want to have fun with the people around me.

LET THE FUN BEGIN!

First on the list of steering away from the *culture of mean* would be to appreciate that everyone is different. You are not going to agree on all things at all times, and that is okay. If each of us were the same, many of us would be unnecessary. While you realize differences, you need to concentrate and stand on your commonality to work well together, which I hope would be top-notch resident care.

Shifting your focus to the positive in others will help you to neglect the negative. It is remarkable how easy it is for the mind to focus only on the negative aspects of almost anything. Unfortunately, we do this with people as well. While we might not be especially comfortable with everyone, we can find common ground and good in others if we choose to look for it.

Here is a little exercise for you. Take a moment and think of three positive aspects of that individual who might rub you the wrong way, and when you see that person in a hallway or at a meeting, or when working side-by-side, concentrate on those three personal positives.

*DON'T BE **THAT** COWORKER*

I have found that wherever miserable people go, there they are! Miserable people cannot get away from themselves. Have you noticed that? The good news is that you can get a break from that individual. You still get to go home. You can go to the beach, the mountains, or the city, whatever you enjoy as you turn your attention away from them and to something fun.

The point is you can get a break from them, but miserable people cannot get a break from themselves. They drag their misery everywhere they go. Knowing that, ultimately, at the end of my shift, wherever I would go, they couldn't, actually gave me a heart for those miserable co-workers stuck with their own company. Instead of letting them make me miserable, I felt pity as I thought of them.

PICK YOUR BATTLES

I always feel sorry for micro-managers. They have their toe in just about everything and never step back to see that others can do something better than they can. The control is stifling, and when you raise your voice to get your way, you wind up being tuned out by good people who only want to do their job. Congratulations, your yelling has just turned you into the boulder I spoke of at the beginning of this chapter.

Instead of micro-managing, ask yourself, *Will this impact patient care, or is this just my obsessive-compulsive workaholism and mico-managing?* More often than not, I think it's just a need to control. Take a step back from this if this description sounds like you. If you don't, you will be like that parent who screams at the top of their lungs at everything. After a while, the children tune out that parent. The children are so used to outbursts of anger and voice of displeasure that they no longer hear that parent.

However, if you're not someone who yells at every little thing, you won't have to yell when you need people's attention. Because you don't always hover over them, you can pull them together and say in a calm and even voice, "We really need to do this in this way because it will help our residents, and it will affect Survey. So I appreciate you doing this in this way." Since you are not constantly pulling them over to correct them, they will receive it and apply it graciously and perhaps gratefully because you're not the hovering manager.

"IT IS BETTER TO SWALLOW THAN TO SPIT"

The above saying is pretty gross, but it is spot on under some circumstances! Sometimes we all have a quick, snarky comeback that comes to mind. That quip could get a laugh and put another person in their place. We've seen that with social media. People are bold at their keyboards as they pour out their sour attitudes to get many others to pile on. And if we can get away with it in person surrounded by people who might stand on our side, we just might let loose right there in the middle of a nurse's station with many others looking on. However, to change the culture, it is far better to swallow those hurtful and most likely inaccurate words and stick to the truth with grace to make an impact in getting what you would like accomplished while uplifting others at the same time. Imagine that!

GETTING TO KNOW YOU

I believe many of our challenges are because we have lost the ability to connect meaningfully as human beings. We no longer make eye contact since we constantly stare at our cellular devices. We spent years masking in areas where you didn't usually wear one, which caused many not to want to talk because it is difficult to speak and even hear somebody else through a mask. Aside from this fact, seeing someone's face is crucial for connection. As I stated in a previous chapter, we *see* each other but don't *look*. We especially don't take time to get to know one another.

Texting or looking at someone's social media, where they only post everything as peachy in their life, does not allow you to get to know them. Here's a little suggestion for you at your next staff meeting. Put individuals into groups of two. Don't pair people together who are already in a click. Pair them with people you don't usually see talking with each other. Have one of the individuals share with the other something about themselves that perhaps they would never have guessed. Maybe before working in your Care Center, they worked in construction, maybe at one point in their life they climbed Mount Everest, perhaps they own horses, whatever that is, they are going to share it with the other individual.

That other individual will then ask five questions about what the other member of your staff shared. Then they'll switch. Give them about ten minutes each to do this. It is a lot of fun, and the volume in the room slowly gets louder and louder as they realize a commonality with each other or learn new things. There's a lot of laughing, and seeing this connection is an awful lot of fun. As the leader, you can then go around the room and ask, "Okay, Mary, can you tell us something about Susie?"

Because they had asked the questions, they can say, "Susie loves to go antiquing, and on one of her antiquing trips, she found a Hummel from the 1940s that she bought for $5, which wound up being worth $10,000!" Hopefully, Susie will not report any attempted burglaries, but you get the point.

INTRODUCING...

I realize that we have all worked with individuals who could bring us to a place of frustration that can cause us to lose our composure. In these instances, we can hurt our integrity before others while disappointing ourselves. So how can you deal with various personalities that you work with who can make your environment difficult? Let's look at some of these personalities and examine some solutions. Once again, rather than making boring lists, I will assign each one a name and then tell you about that individual and what you can do to be a change agent.

1. Valerie Venter uses someone, it doesn't matter who, as a sounding board to dump off all her complaints. Once she is done venting, Valerie will feel light and airy. However, the person she dumped it on is now angry and frustrated and carrying a load they didn't have before they walked through your facility's doors.

What do you do about Valerie Venter? You can approach her and say, "I understand you have some concerns about *such and such*. I'm very curious to know your thoughts on this. What I would like you to do is, instead of going to various people who can't help in the situation, which can perhaps leave them just as frustrated as you are, I'd like you to write out what the challenge is and then give me three suggested solutions. Please put that on my desk, and I will consider them."

With the above approach, Valerie knows you are taking her concern seriously, and if somebody's having a bad day, she is not passing any added burdens on to them. Having her place her concern on your desk rather than coming up to you every five minutes with what isn't urgent is better. Valerie might have a valid concern and already have a good solution. You won't know unless you allow her to express it. If she doesn't have solutions, all she is doing is complaining, and this assignment exposes that. However, if she doesn't have any solutions, it should stop her from constantly passing that toxic energy on to others because she is aware that you know she's doing it.

2. Terry Topthis believes no one has it as bad, no one does it as good, no one has as much, and no one has seen all that he has, which means Terry is a pro at playing the *Can-You-Top-This* game. If you say you hiked to the top of Mount Saint Helens, he will say he hiked to the tip of Mount Rainier. If you say you just won $400 on a scratch off lottery ticket someone put in your birthday card, he will tell you he won $4,000 on one he picked up from the ground while walking his dog. People like Terry could drive you crazy if you let them. I think just a change in response is needed.

When people play the *Can-You-Top-This* game, I imagine they don't feel very good about themselves and, sadly, need a lot of affirmation. I think it is unfortunate to have to diminish other people to make yourself feel better. I feel sorry for people like this and cannot be angry with them. My comeback would be, "Wow, that's cool that you hiked Mount Rainier, maybe one day I'll try to do that, but for now, I'm pretty proud of my Mount Saint Helens hike!" It's all good. Grumbling about Terry will spoil your day and the day of those you complain to about him. Just chuckle to yourself and feel sorry that that's what he has to do to make himself feel better.

3. Freddy Faultfinder points the finger constantly at what other people do or say that he thinks is wrong, yet he refuses to see his flaws. Freddy is someone who absolutely cannot take constructive criticism. He might even turn things around and make the conversation about you! If there's an issue with Freddy, he might say it is your fault. What do we do with the Freddy fault finder? Don't take it personally.

The fact is you are not a human doing. You are a human being. If you make a mistake, own it. But don't waste your time if you realize an individual like Freddy cannot be reasoned with. It is better to listen graciously and say, "I'll consider that." And then let it go! It is better to do this than attempt to point out the flaws in this individual, who probably has many.

If there are challenges for Freddie that need to be communicated, communicate them. If he tries to move you to your faults, simply state, "I will be glad to hear your thoughts on that in a minute. However, let's stay focused and finish our conversation on this particular challenge we need to address."

The foremost thing to consider, especially if you are in leadership, is if you could be a Freddy Faultfinder. Is it possible that you are pointing out the flaws of everybody else, but you're not very honest about your own? Are you approachable? Can people be candid with you about your faults? Do you have a tough time taking constructive criticism? Could it be time for a little bit of introspection?

Each of us has areas where we can improve; if we're not open to that improvement, we will never grow and will not move forward. Unfortunately, we will wind up being stagnant or even take steps backward. That's not where you want to be. Take some time and consider if you can be a Freddy Faultfinder, and think about the adjustments you might need to make.

4. Connor Complainer will obsess over his concerns or challenges. Unlike a *Valerie Venter*, who will share her frustrations and feels better afterward, when Connor vents to others, he becomes more heated! The intensity grows each time he discusses the challenge with another person. He would rather ruminate instead of letting it go. After Connor complains to others, everyone around him feels like they're walking on eggshells because the more he talks about it, the angrier he becomes.

My suggestion for Connor Complainer is the same as for a *Valerie Venter*. Request that he jot down his concern and offer three solutions. Remind him that sometimes people come to work and have many of their own challenges and might want a break, so if he has a challenge he is frustrated about, have him come to you by way of a written concern with three solutions, and on your desk it goes. You never know what Connor can develop if he is thinking about it that much. He might solve it or realize he doesn't have a solution and will keep it to himself.

5. Yanni Yeahbut is someone who does not honestly want a solution. This individual, no matter what solution you give him, the response will be, "Yeah, but…" and he is off and running with another excuse as to why your suggested solution won't work. If you have ever counseled others, you have encountered a Yanni Yeahbut. They only want to consume your time and reveal their mind.

You can ask Yanni, "Other than this particular challenge, is there anything else you can think of that is also bothering you about working here?"

Since Yanni doesn't believe you can actually solve it, he will say, "No, that's it!" Now, you might have a solution on the spot, and if you offer that solution, he says, as a way to get out of doing what you said, "Yeah, but..."

You can then tell Yanni, "See, I gave you a solution, and you gave me another, *yeah, but* so I have a feeling you really don't want an answer to the concern. So what I want you to do is write out the challenge fully and give me three solutions, then put it on my desk, and I'll consider them." End of story. Then look at it in your time. Who knows, maybe Yanni will have an epiphany!

6. Peggy Pessimist is negative regarding just about everything! Even if it's good, she still finds a way to be negative about it. Her negativity then spreads like cancer. For example, if your center was newly remodeled, she may look at the carpeting and complain about how much she hates it. Her negativity can then bring other people down.

I would then approach Peggy and say, "Peggy, I understand you don't like the carpet. How about we look at it together and give me three things you do like about it." Remember the old sales axiom. *She who talks first loses!* Do not peep until she gives you three things that she does like. She might say the room smells better. You can reply, "Very true, new carpet smells excellent. Give me something else."

She might then reply, "It does make the room look bigger."

Encouragingly you can say, "That's right, who doesn't like a larger room? Give me one more."

She might return with, "It doesn't have any stains all over it."

To which you can reply, "Absolutely, true! The new carpet doesn't have any stains. So, Peggy, you like the smell, how it makes the room look bigger, and that it's stain free since it's brand new. Please do me a favor. Every time you come in, I want you to think about the three good things you just told me you liked."

All this is to say that whenever Peggy Pessimist expresses her pessimism, ask her for three positive things no matter the situation. Give her a big smile and say, "Good job! Thanks so much."

Sometimes people do not know they are a *Peggy Pessimist* or a *Negative Nelly*. There might have been things in their life that brought them to that place. Sometimes they need somebody else on the outside with a smile to help turn that thinking around.

7. Lizzy Lazy does the absolute minimum amount of work required and, at the same time, will work quite hard to gain sympathy for over-the-top excuses to unload her work on others. Lizzy could very well impact the ability to keep good employees. You might look down the hallway one way, turn around and look down the other, and see that everything seems perfectly fine with all your residents happy and everything in order. But the key is how it got that way.

Did it get that way on the backs of other staff members who are the worker bees while there is one slacker? If that slacker isn't dealt with, those who do work hard to pick up where Lizzy refuses will become discouraged. Eventually, they grumble, "Why am I busting my tail as she gets the credit?"

How do we handle Lizzy Lazy? When delegating, state, "If anyone here thinks they'll have difficulty completing the task, please let me know right now." Most of the time, Lizzy will not want to express to management what she told her coworkers to get out of doing her job. The fact is she just doesn't want to do it.

Therefore by making Lizzy Lazy directly accountable to you by admitting that she's unable, she will probably keep silent and get it done since the worker bees can then say, "Why didn't you tell the Charge Nurse who asked?" Eventually, Lizzy will be found out, and a chat needs to happen to explain that if she cannot handle her workload, perhaps a different position would be more appropriate.

8. Fanny Favorite purposefully builds a powerful social clique similar to *Connie Control* in a previous chapter. She will overtly favor certain people, usually those who feel more comfortable as followers than leaders. Favoritism is not a good dynamic because it leaves others outside the clique. However, the exercise I suggested earlier that you can use during one of your meetings allows people to get to know each other. Therefore, some staff members in the clique might find much more in common with people outside of that dynamic while not neglecting their relationship with Fanny. Unite your Care Center under your Care Center's name, not a specific, dominant personality. The goal is to *leave no staff member behind!*

9. Gus Gossip engages in destructive, hurtful behavior that can pin people against each other. Gossip is a cancer to any organization. Gossip will undermine trust among employees and foster a terrible sense of paranoia. For example, suppose you are conducting a staff meeting, and someone sitting across the room notices Gus Gossip lean over and whisper something to someone. They then see the other person whisper something back. Suddenly, they both begin laughing. Because people know Gus is a gossip, paranoia can begin. People looking on might think Gus is laughing with another individual about them. That onlooker then tells someone else, "Did you see how Gus was probably spreading lies about me at the meeting this morning?" And off it goes!

And yet, the conversation might have been as innocuous as Gus saying, "Do you have a pen? Mine just died."

To which the other person might have said, "Just type it in your phone."

To which Gus responds, "My phone's dead too!" Then they both laugh.

However, it is not a laughing matter for the onlooker who knows that Gus gossips. Because gossip is so destructive to any organization, I will fully address this topic in various ways throughout the next chapter.

WORK IN THEIR SHOES

While leaders must come alongside those they lead, they must also *work* alongside those they wish to lead. If you are a leader in your organization, feel free to take the opportunity to work next to various individuals with differing positions. If you're at the top, understanding how your staff members go about their day is a good idea. Understanding your staff's struggles, training, malfunctioning equipment, and successes will help you be a better leader and a more appropriate problem solver. It will also help you identify individuals matching the particular dynamics of the challenged co-workers described.

When you shadow other employees, do not correct them as they go about their duties unless it is something vital that cannot wait. In that case, be diplomatic so they feel comfortable with you as you continue to work together. When you are shadowing, it is simply a time for you to understand their position and the challenges they might face and to hear their solutions, if any.

Though you might not hold a credential in each position, make an effort to be alongside that individual as much as possible. I suggest you do this with your nursing staff, food services, maintenance, housekeeping, etc. The information you can glean as you work each position will provide a wealth of knowledge and save you a lot of money on consultants. You might find out that certain pieces of equipment aren't working well. The staff might have devised a way to sidestep it such that it could be hazardous to them rather than taking the time to alert management. It's kind of the, *We've always done it this way* mentality. In the next chapter, I will show you how your staff members are your greatest asset if you weren't already aware!

QUESTIONS FOR THOUGHT

1. As you read the list of various personalities, could any apply to some of your employees? Will your approach change in your response to them? If so, how?
2. Could there be hidden frustrations among your staff members? Are you willing to find out what they might be? Are you willing to make changes if necessary?
3. Do you suffocate your employees by micro-managing them? If so, why don't you trust them enough to do the job for which you hired them? Is it time to take a step back and trust those you chose to hire?
4. Have you taken time to work in the shoes of the varying individuals among your staff? What did you learn about their position and needs if you did? What

did you change either in your Center or management style?

5. Are you guilty of being a boulder that crushes as it rolls downhill? If so, have you made amends with those whose spirit you crushed?

8. Disembarking from the Gossip Train

Previously, I touched on how the behavior of a *Gus Gossip* can be very destructive to your Care Center. However, we must admit because we're human that, we have all been guilty of being a *Gus Gossip*. The destructive nature of gossip is that it can lead to confrontations. Workplace confrontations can then lead to bad press, lawsuits, and even career loss.

There are a few things to be mindful of when considering the topic of gossip. Not to make you paranoid, but in this day and age, you should always assume someone is watching you, listening to you, or even recording you. I hate to say that, but it is better to be safe than sorry.

Never was the awareness of being watched and listened to more evident than one evening in Assisted Living when I was standing before my cart and about to begin my evening med pass. I heard a little commotion and looked down the hallway to see two CNAs creating a lot of heat between each other but not much light. I would have gotten the most hilarious picture if I had a camera.

Three female residents sitting at the puzzle-table (what I would affectionately refer to as *the petri dish*) were leaning back in their chairs as far as they could to listen as best they could to the two CNAs arguing directly behind them. The CNAs were easily in earshot of everybody. Taking a deep breath and slightly shaking my head, I quickly locked up my cart, strolled close to the angry coworkers, and, with a slight grin, I said, "Ladies, let's take a little walk where we can talk a little more privately." We went into the empty dining room and, with a smile, I said, "*Geez Louise*, what is going on with you guys?"

The one angrily stated, "She just up and disappeared on me. I hate when that happens. I was looking all over the place for her because I needed help. I'm not cleaning all this up alone!"

To which the other one said, "I didn't know you didn't hear me say where I went. I grabbed all the napkins and other stuff and brought them upstairs to get the laundry going. I didn't think you would have enough time to be able to do it so I decided to do it for you! I didn't know you didn't hear me."

The truth is, the whole thing was an unfortunate misunderstanding. Those two CNAs generally got along great, so it surprised me that their argument got so heated. They wound up hugging it out, and after a good night of hard work, I suggested that I treat them to some caffeine at our local coffee shop that was open until midnight. They thought that sounded great, and we all returned to work without incident. The whole thing was resolved in about five minutes.

However, consider the residents sitting around *the petri dish*. That angry disagreement between those two co-workers was a bit of excitement, and you don't keep that kind of unrest to yourself! Can you imagine those residents as they spoke to their family members over the telephone? Everyone has played the telephone game. Perhaps their call might have gone like this, "You had to see these two CNAs going at it! They were furious! Judy had to separate them and take them into the dining room, where I think I heard someone throw a plate! Judy finally got them to calm down. But it took a while."

Then, of course, that family member talks to other family members. How would *that* conversation go? "I'm really worried about Mom being in that Care Center with that crazy nursing staff. It sounds like they have a lot of anger issues over there. Do you think it's time to pull Mom out?" And so it goes.

The following conversation could happen when one of the resident's family members is at the grocery store and just happens to run into a friend with a question. "Your Mom is at that Care Center by you. How does she like it there?"

The family member's answer might be, "Well, I used to think it was good, but it seems the staff doesn't get along very well over there. A couple of other residents told me the same thing! Perhaps you should consider elsewhere for now." Not good.

Something else about the two staff members arguing with eavesdropping residents nearby is highly unsettling. The fact that they can forget their surroundings to the point of having a heated disagreement with residents in earshot shows that there is a disconnect from the reality of the uniqueness of that workspace. Unfortunately, it is evidence that our residents have become like fixtures instead of human beings who can pass on some destructive and inaccurate information through gossip.

Something else happens when residents see tension between staff members. Each resident will take sides. And if that particular resident isn't on your side if you're in that situation, that can negatively impact your workplace success. A resident who doesn't like you because they believe something untrue about you can make your working environment pretty miserable. We have to be extremely careful. As the POA for a loved one for ten years, I could tell that not only was Clarence a fixture for some of those who worked there, but because I visited him so often, I was as well, and they would drop their guard and say all kinds of things to each other thinking we weren't paying attention. When in fact, our ears are quite perked up!

HEADS UP!

Though I know it is spoken about during training, I can tell you without flinching it has gone in one ear and out the other for many who work in Care Centers. It would be best to remember that the residents and their families are not there to meet your staff member's or your emotional needs. Confiding with a resident or their family about work-related frustrations or personal or personnel issues is like gasoline to a wildfire. It will spread explosively and become entirely out of control. And it won't be easy to put out.

What impact could divulging painful or difficult personal or personnel issues have on a resident? While you might feel better after venting, your resident can see it differently. I remember walking into a room as I passed meds to a particular resident who asked me, "Is Annie alright?" (Of course, the names have been changed to protect the guilty.)

Taken aback a bit, I said, "Of course, Annie's okay. Annie is fine. Why?"

"Well," my resident said with a troubled look, "I'm afraid for her. She got into a fight with that guy she's living with. He doesn't seem like a very nice man. I'm really afraid for her safety!"

I was stunned at how much she knew about the situation with Annie. But I was even more stunned that Annie was sharing this private information with one of the residents! The stress on this older woman's face was palpable. This woman had enough challenges of her own; she did not need any of our staff dumping theirs on her so they could feel light and airy for the rest of the day. I attempted to give her peace by replying, "No, everything is fine."

"Oh, I'm so thankful. I'm so relieved," my resident said as a weight she didn't need in the first place lifted.

Your residents don't need to carry your stressors or the staff's. They have enough of their own! Everyone needs to vent about personal life or workplace challenges, which is understandable, but perhaps your friends, family, a counselor, or clergy would be a better place to start.

COWORKERS BULLY?

You might find this hard to believe, but co-workers can also bully each other just as a resident can bully another resident. Shocking, I know. I mentioned that I had worked briefly in hospice, long-term care, and rehab as a CNA and was then promoted to a Med Tech and moved into Assisted Living. While I waited for my training day on the medication cart that I spoke of in a previous chapter, my DON asked me to fulfill some CNA tasks in Assisted Living until then. These tasks included responsibilities in the dining room and kitchen. The DON told me she would have the other CNAs show me the ropes. I then found myself relying on two women who I quickly realized didn't like me.

I have no idea why they didn't like me, especially since they had just met me! I had never even had a conversation with either of them. Nevertheless, they chose to hold that position.

The first night I was in the kitchen, I was unsure what to do, so I asked some questions and noticed the CNA go out of her way to refuse to help me. She would not answer any of my questions. Without any eye contact, she said, "You're pretty smart. You'll figure it out."

I said, "But aren't you supposed to show me what I'm to do and where things are?"

She said, "Well, I have other things right now." I could tell she was deliberately trying to sabotage my job. That is bullying! Of course, I did figure it out.

Eventually, those two CNAs not only saw that I could *figure it out* but also realized that I had a fierce work ethic and was willing to do what it took to get the job done. After they got to know me, which I believe made the difference, they became very friendly with me and even admitted and laughed about how they tried to sabotage me. While I chuckled on the outside, I took note on the inside as to how these two mature women in their sixties could act so childishly. But as we've learned, bullies have no age limits.

THINK FIRST!

Before you talk about another staff member, ask yourself, "Is what I am going to say about that other person friendly, fair, factual, or forgiving?" If the answer to any of those is, *No*, then forget it. Don't even let it come out of your mouth. And not only that, don't listen to it! If people know you have a standard in that you won't listen to gossip, they won't share it with you.

Take a step back and think about the impact it would have on your organization if people used that filter and asked themselves, "Is it friendly, fair, factual, or forgiving?" then, realizing it might not be, they'd forget about sharing it. If you need to, as I did in the highly trafficked Assisted Living office, type that out, laminate it, and post it. And I'd sure appreciate you letting folks know you found it in this book if you do. Joking aside, the phrase, *think before you speak* has never been so imperative!

GOOD GOSSIP

Let's acknowledge the fact that people love to talk about others. Reality shows wouldn't be popular if this weren't the case. People love to peer into other people's lives. Therefore, if gossip is unavoidable, how do we change it from bad gossip to good gossip? Is that even possible? I believe it is, and I will now share ways to foster *good gossip* in your Care Center to help folks unite.

A fun suggestion to get things started in the quest to bring folks together through good gossip would be that you have at the nurse's station a photo feature entitled, *Who Can This Be?* The person in the photograph should not be easily recognizable. Perhaps the co-worker is in a costume, a uniform, or as a small child. You can then keep a jar in the nurse's station, where other staff members write the name of the person they thought it was. The following month you can then reveal the top three picks. You can then share who it was, and a different person can have their picture up the next month. Suddenly people are walking past each other, saying, "I think that's you." Or, "Who do you think that is?" It's uplifting and can bring people together. It can also help people get to know each other. Again that is vital because once the two women who bullied me in Assisted Living got to know me, we had a good working relationship.

OPPORTUNITIES FOR UNITY

While some folks might feel my next suggestion is a bit old-fashioned, you can use it to bring people together if done effectively. I am talking about your Care Center having a newsletter. For my example, I'm going to title it *Camaraderie*. The newsletter can be printed, or if you want to save paper, something you can email to everyone or put up on the bulletin board. However, I highly suggest printing it because there's something about having it physically in your hands when your name is on it. It is something physical you can show someone else, which is exciting, especially when it has your proud moments.

The newsletter entitled *Camaraderie* can have a variety of contributors, or you can enlist one person from your staff to interview different people. You can have a section on *Employee Fun Facts.* Perhaps it states, "Sam is a published writer," or "Susie used to be a semi-truck driver."

You can have what you could call a *Hot Tip* section. For example, it can read:

> A lower-pitched voice is easier to hear. Consider dropping your vocal pitch down a notch to see if that helps your resident hear you more easily when chatting.

The above suggestion was something I noticed with Clarence. He could easily hear my husband, who didn't talk very loudly, but sometimes Clarence couldn't hear me. I realized he would have no problem hearing me if I just lowered my pitch. In any event, you can have different people suggest what they feel would be a good *Hot Tip.*

Include a *Volunteer of the Month* section that could read:

> Thanks to Sam for volunteering this month to read to our residents.

> Thanks to Susie for volunteering her time to do some sewing repairs.

The person who extends the *thank you* should be the individual who holds the highest position in your organization. Having this high-level person thank the individual lets those you are thanking know that the good they do is noticed by more than just their immediate coworkers. People appreciate when you acknowledge their notable additions to your Center. Acknowledging and thanking your staff members helps with longevity. People who feel appreciated stay with organizations that recognize their hard or extra work.

Encouraging Words can be another section. A little encouragement goes a long way. Maybe you can share something like the Panama Canal Builders song, one of my favorites. It is one I identify with very personally:

> *Got any rivers they say are uncrossable,*
> *Got any tunnels they say can't tunnel through?*
> *We specialize in the wholly impossible,*
> *Doing the things they say you can't do.*

There can also be an *Above & Beyond* section. Once again, this section will be written by the individual with the highest position in your organization. It could read:

> Mary noticed Claudia needed extra help and offered a hand without being asked. Way to look out for each other, Mary! Thank you for going above and beyond!
>
> After Bob had clocked out, he noticed one of our residents in the dining room feeling sad. He sat with him for a while until he felt better. Way to go above and beyond, Bob!

Have a section to congratulate people on things you know they've been working on. Or you can have their special occasions in your newsletter, like birthdays, weddings, birth announcements, special graduations, or anniversaries. It can read:

> Don't forget to congratulate William for officially becoming an RN!
>
> Remember to congratulate Mary for finishing top ten in a marathon last month.

Putting announcements like the above into your newsletter demonstrates to your staff that you take a personal interest in the good things that happened for people in your Care Center. It promotes good gossip in their conversation.

For new folks who come into your Center, you can have a *Say Hello* section to make them feel welcome and allow others to get to know them better. For example, it can read:

> Say hello to Susie, our newest CNA in rehab. She comes to us with ten years of experience, has a great sense of humor, and loves horseback riding, concert going, and knitting.

Staff members who also have those shared interests now have a connection with your new employee.

I think it's also important to reward people when they're speaking positively about your organization outside of the Center. You can have a referral rewards program and offer a spiff for staff members who refer clients to your Care Center. It can read:

> Mary suggested Mrs. Jones come and check us out. Now that Mrs. Jones joins us as one of our fabulous new residents as our thank you to Mary, we hope she'll enjoy spending her special *Resident Referral Reward*! Thank you so much, Mary!

We are very concerned about our residents' health but should also let our staff members know we're concerned about their health. Perhaps including *Health Tips* like:

> Staying hydrated will help you stay more alert. When you're feeling tired, you just might be a little dehydrated. Pure water is better than sugary stuff. So drink up!

Working at a Care Center is unique since others live in your workplace, which can make it even more stressful. So offer some *Stress Relievers*, perhaps suggesting:

> Walking in the fresh air is a great way to relieve stress. Maybe sometime this week, grab a few co-workers and stroll around the lake. Just remember to talk about anything but work!

You can have a *Community Events* or *Local News* section for your newsletter. Perhaps you include something new happening in your community or something exciting at your Care Center. You can also tell folks what businesses have helped or donated things like blankets or other items. When other businesses see their competitor's name in your newsletter and what they donated for the elderly or infirm, they might just want to join in!

A *Problem Solved* column in the newsletter is a great way to show your employees that you care about their thoughts and ideas. People who work with you might have a wealth of experience in other areas. What's interesting is I worked at that Care Center and saw so many things that could be made better simply because I had the eyes to see them because of my unique training, background, and experience. Unfortunately, management didn't take my suggestion to create a special training program seriously because I was *just a*

CNA in their eyes. This belittling thinking is a tragic mistake. One I think my years of success with *LPNequip.org* has proved.

You might have people who work at your Care Center with family who own a restaurant chain. This individual might be working in maintenance, and every time they walk through your dining room, they have a wealth of knowledge and experience for ideas of how things could be made more streamlined. Unfortunately, you won't value their voice in other areas because you only view them as *just a maintenance person*. Well, it's time to give everyone a voice and, again, save a fortune on consultants!

Have a box somewhere that is accessible where staff members can write out how they met a challenge they faced. They can jot what they did onto a note card and place it in the box. Management can then review them. You will quickly realize who your ideas people are and also the ones with a valuable creative side. If a particular position should open in your Care Center, you might have someone appropriate for it right under your nose, even though they currently work in a different department.

If you wind up using a suggestion from that box, ensure the employee gets acknowledgment for their solution by noting it in your newsletter. This mention will encourage more staff members to utilize your suggestion box. They can include something learned in a class, at a previous position elsewhere, or from personal experience. Again it's much better to listen to the ideas and thoughts of people who work with you before spending a fortune on consultants or headhunters.

QUESTIONS FOR THOUGHT

1. Do you have a newsletter or something like it? Has it helped to bring your staff together?
2. Have you or your staff members crossed a line to sharing personal or personnel information with residents? How can you rectify this?
3. Are you aware of a bullying situation among your staff members? If so, what will you do to help?
4. Will you employ the *friendly, fair, factual, or forgiving* question to filter what you might share with others? Could this be helpful for your staff members?
5. How much money can you save on consultants by allowing your staff to share their thoughts, opinions, or ideas freely?

9. Checking Your Baggage at the Door

Throughout this, the shortest chapter, I want to address something that can sabotage your goal of becoming a change agent for good in your Care Center. I think it is necessary to address the fact that sometimes we can drag our baggage or bad day from our personal life into the home of the individuals who rely on our compassionate care.

PERSPECTIVE IS KEY

If you are honest with yourself, what do you believe runs through your coworker's minds when you walk through the doors of your Care Center as soon as they lay eyes on you? Do you believe they are thinking, *Oh, thank goodness* (insert your name) *is here!* Or are they thinking, *Oh no,* (insert your name) *is here!* The answer could hit you like a warm blanket or a cold rag. It's up to you.

Now take a moment and consider what goes through *your* mind when you walk through the doors of your Care Center. Are your thoughts positive, or are they negative? Are you rolling your eyes before you walk through your Care Center doors, or are you telling yourself, "It is a new day with new opportunities!"

If you tend to roll your eyes, I will pose to you the same question I posed to the Administrator I mentioned in an earlier chapter. *Would you trade your worst day for any of your resident's best days?* I am an absolute believer that gratitude can replace grumbling. It is often a lot easier to look at the negative things of life, or the things we think will go wrong than what is true and good. A proper perspective can prompt compassion for our residents, patience with our coworkers, and an awareness that we work in the home of others.

Again, working in a Care Facility is quite a unique setting. It is one that certainly presents its challenges. Why would I mention that once again in this book and at this juncture? Imagine you are sitting in your living room, and I burst through the door complaining, grumbling, and angry as I grab a coffee while whining about this or that. And there you are, just trying to have a peaceful moment. You don't feel well. Your body hurts physically, and you would just like a little peace. You also feel sad as you think about how things and people used to be in your life years ago. Our eyes connect, and I flash you a little smile, but as soon as my eyes turn from you, my expression changes, and my irritation is evident. You know I don't want to be in your home. But you're stuck with me.

How would you feel about an individual who burst on the scene like that, conscious that their presence can change the mood of a room? Powerful personalities, like those in leadership, can do that. But was the change in the room for the better all around? What would it be like for you to have to listen to someone bark at other people in your living room all day? When considering it just that way, it certainly can shine a different light on your workplace attitude.

However, what if I walked into your home at least fifteen minutes before I needed to be there so that I could say a proper *hello* and greet you with a genuine smile that didn't fade as soon as we broke eye contact? What if I did that as part of my concern for you, and you knew it? What if, before I walked through those doors, no matter how heavy my heart was, I considered yours heavier and, therefore, I felt it was my duty to make yours lighter? What if you had helpers I was to oversee, and as soon as I saw them, I thanked them for a job well done and then expressed how much I appreciated their kind care for you? Now, think for a moment. Which scenario fits you?

WHAT IF?

But what if you can't shake that bad day? What if you can't shake your sour attitude? What if your baggage feels like a chain around your ankle as you drag it through the doors of your Care Center? Are these personal challenges that you're having right now? Tell someone. Talk to someone. Get counseling. Please, talk with a friend, family member, counselor, or clergy member, but don't let it go. Because perhaps you need a change of perspective.

But what if you still, no matter what, cannot kick your sour attitude when you walk through the doors of your Care Center? What if it suddenly occurs to you that the sour mood is coming from your workplace? Is this something that can be fixed? Are there people who are aware of the challenges? Can you talk to people in higher positions than you to help make some adjustments and changes to make things better? If those things happen and changes are made, but you still feel like a *square peg in a round hole*, then perhaps it's time to ask yourself if your current position is a stepping stone instead of a career.

Every job-related experience we have helps us in the future. I never imagined that the variety of career choices and experiences I have had would result in the incredible fun I'm having at this stage of my life. As you will find in the next section, I knew my time at the Care Center was temporary. I was not doing it for my career or advancement somewhere else. Yet I had no idea how it would impact what I now do.

If you walk through the doors, grumbling every moment, and you can't shake the *square peg in a round hole* feeling, though it isn't easy, take time and consider if your position at the Care Center is right for you. It is far better to step aside and allow someone to hold that position who is eager and thankful for it and will make a positive impact than someone miserable and who feels burnt out. It's the difference between how I viewed passing meds as a newly installed Med Tech and the outgoing nurse who viewed the residents as *Night of the Living Dead*. It makes a difference to the individual doing the work, the co-workers, and of course, it all impacts the quality of care for your residents.

Again, we have the responsibility and the power to impact our environment for good. I hope you will apply what you've learned in this three-chapter section so that you never again walk through the doors of any organization rolling your eyes and instead will have a positive attitude. If this is your mindset, you will significantly impact many people for good wherever you go.

QUESTIONS FOR THOUGHT

1. What is my attitude toward the Care Center?
2. What is my attitude toward my coworkers?
3. What is my attitude toward the residents?
4. Do I need an attitude adjustment?
5. Have I allowed my co-workers the opportunity to be positive change agents by allowing them to express ideas and a vision? Could some of the most unlikely co-workers hold the answer to some of the biggest challenges? Am I open to their solutions?

SECTION FOUR

A Commonsense Approach To Emotional Trauma And Why We Ask, Why?

10. Emotional Trauma Basics

There is a growing prevalence in our culture and Care Centers of people having difficulty unpacking emotionally painful past experiences. This emotional stress can affect the staff and residents you serve. Throughout this last segment, I hope you will recognize the dynamics of emotional trauma in others and perhaps even yourself for greater understanding. If you can relate, I hope the information outlined in these last chapters will help you to thrive so that you can be a helper to many others instead of feeling helpless with your emotional pain or that of another person.

It seems that despair is on the rise, as well as suicide rates in the United States. In 2021, according to the Centers for Disease Control (CDC), over forty-eight thousand Americans have died by suicide with 1.7 million attempts. Many people in our society and culture feel a sense of hopelessness and despair for various reasons. Therefore, this is a vital topic to address in this final segment since it does indeed affect your residents and staff members.

WHY ME?

You might be asking why I would be someone who would speak on such a topic. I have a unique and intimate perspective on emotional trauma since I suffered from post-traumatic stress and obsessive-compulsive disorders for many years. My home life was challenging for me throughout my childhood as I was often referred to as "*the accident*." While growing up, I have no memory of ever being comforted when frightened, in pain, or upset, and the words *I love you* were never uttered. Life outside the home wasn't much better in my tough neighborhood until I hit high school and moved to another community.

My father had challenges with anger and alcohol. That is an explosive combination. One that children don't fully understand. When children live in an alcoholic home, two things are evident. One is that it is okay to lie about why people can't come over or why you have a particular bruise. Secrets also become a substantial part of your life because there's an incredible amount of shame and fear associated with living in that environment. Children who live with lies, secrets, and intense fear, as if constantly walking on eggshells, do not usually make the most emotionally healthy adults.

Children living in highly stressful physical and emotional survival modes are generally unsuccessful scholastically as concentration, a necessity for success, is quite tricky. For me, what added to that mix was that I also had terrible eyesight and could not see the chalkboard, even with corrective lenses. Unfortunately, when my poor vision was realized as a first grader, I had an eye doctor who did not believe me when I told him, through tears, that I still couldn't see the big "*E*," and for some odd reason, he refused to give me a strong enough prescription for my eyeglasses. Therefore, I tanked as a student, especially since, in the 1970s, the *dumb kids*, who I was thought to be, were made to sit in the back of the class!

I felt little to zero self-worth. Believing what others said, for many years, I viewed myself as a dumb mistake—simply as a miserable accident. However, I certainly know now that there are scores of people whose lives I have impacted through my own who would certainly take issue with that thinking.

Other events and circumstances made my formative years painful and palpably lonely, but what I've offered thus far is enough to give you a snapshot. I must also confess that this is the first time I have ever shared such details about my life in any of my books or other writings. In all candor, I am not my favorite subject. I am not sharing these things in this work to create an autobiography. I share this information with the hope of helping others to heal and become more effective. If readers find the Light at the end of their tunnel through this work, I am grateful I can play a small part in that journey.

Aside from the fact that I have intimate knowledge of emotional trauma, having suffered from post-traumatic stress, obsessive-compulsive disorders, and palpable fears, a few other things qualify me to speak on the topic. I have been a Certified Lay Counselor since 2010, and I've been serving as the Crisis Care Counselor in my fire department as a volunteer since 2017.

EMOTIONAL TRAUMA TRAINING

When my fire chief requested that I also volunteer as the Crisis Care Counselor in our department, he wanted to be confident I felt comfortable and equipped in that role. Therefore he sent me to a sixteen-hour certification training on emotional trauma specifically for First Responders. It was the most prolonged sixteen hours I think I have ever spent. The thought that ran through my mind at the end of it was, *Yup, there's nothing quite like getting emotional trauma from your emotional trauma course!* But the reason for that is most likely not what you might think.

The instructor spoke about a thousand miles per second with a completely monotone voice. She made no eye contact with her participants, nor did she interact. There were no discussion times during her *lecturing*. There were no question-and-answer sessions. She did not stop talking until it was time for a break. With each break, her attendance numbers dwindled. As someone who teaches communication and presentation skills, I wanted to jump out of the window, but I couldn't. There were none.

As I reflect upon that class and consider the individuals in the room, I will never forget a firefighter who wore a t-shirt memorializing one of his fallen comrades. That young man attended that class for answers; sadly, the only thing he got from the presenter was cold erudition. Before every factoid we received in this highly cerebral presentation, she prefaced it with, "The science says...". In fact, that presenter used the phrase *the science says* so often that it became almost a nonsense word, in the same way as if you repeatedly repeated the word *iron*.

"*THE* SCIENCE *SAYS?*"

However, let's take a step back and think about her preface, *the science says*, and how it is inaccurate and downright silly, especially regarding emotional trauma. Bear with me as I explain. There is a method to my madness. And it is significant.

You see, *science* doesn't *say* anything. *Science* is a discipline. It is confined to that which is observable and repeatable. That is the discipline of science. It is simply a means, one of many, that helps us to arrive at what is true. Science is not an end-all because though the scientific process of observation and repeatability is foundational, those who conduct scientific inquiries can slip in their methods. Just read the following excerpt from an article entitled, *Beware Those Scientific Studies—Most are Wrong, Researcher Warns*:

> Washington (AFP) - A few years ago, two researchers... touched on a known but persistent problem in the research world: too few studies have large enough samples to support generalized conclusions.

> But pressure on researchers, competition between journals and the media's insatiable appetite for new studies announcing revolutionary breakthroughs has meant such articles continue to be published.
>
> "The majority of papers that get published, even in serious journals, are pretty sloppy," said John Ioannidis, professor of medicine at Stanford University, who specializes in the study of scientific studies.
>
> This sworn enemy of bad research published a widely cited article in 2005 entitled: *Why Most Published Research Findings Are False.*[2]

As a true science lover, the above is infuriating yet understandable. We see it all the time. A scientist or researcher will excitedly and immediately go to the media before all the cameras and microphones with a *find*. They will then send their *discovery* out for peer review (Which is backward. It should be peer review first, then media.), and when, during the peer review process, they find that the *find* isn't one, the paper is quietly retracted. Yet the news story remains.

Consider the following article pointing out how the *Fall of Top US Scientists Points to Ethics Gap in Research*:

> Three prominent US scientists have been pushed to resign over the past ten days after damning revelations about their methods, a sign of greater vigilance and decreasing tolerance for misconduct within the research community.

---

[2]*https://phys.org/news/2018-07-beware-scientific-studiesmost-wrong.html*

> "The good news is that we are finally starting to see a lot of these cases become public," said Ivan Oransky co-founder of the site Retraction Watch,[3] a project of the Center for Scientific Integrity that keeps tabs on retractions of research articles in thousands of journals.
>
> Oransky told AFP that what has emerged so far is only the tip of the iceberg.
>
> The problem, he said, is that scientists, and supporters of science, have often been unwilling to raise such controversies. But silence only encourages bad behavior, he argued.[4]

Remembering that the discipline of science is confined to that which is observable and repeatable, I will share the following disheartening and shocking snippet from an article in 2020 written about someone who should have known better.

> Frances Arnold, an American scientist and winner of the Nobel Prize in chemistry, retracted a paper published last year after admitting to faulty research.
>
> The award-winning scientist said in a series of tweets Thursday that the work had not been "reproducible" and that she had been "very busy" when the paper was submitted. Arnold added she "did not do my job well."[5]

If you feel perhaps 2020 is a bit too long ago, how about the following from July 19, 2023?

---

[3] For some rather eye-opening articles see: https://retractionwatch.com/

[4] https://phys.org/news/2018-09-fall-scientists-ethics-gap.html

[5] https://www.foxnews.com/science/nobel-prize-winning-scientist-retracts-paper

> *Stanford President to Resign After Investigation Finds He Failed To 'Decisively And Forthrightly' Correct Research*
>
> In an abrupt turn, Stanford president and renowned neuroscientist Marc Tessier-Lavigne announced Wednesday that he will step down as the university's leader. His resignation came after he learned the results of an extensive investigation into his past research, which confirmed data manipulation in scientific papers that he co-authored and found that he took insufficient steps to correct them.[6]

Tragically, most folks never see the multitude of retractions or corrections that could impact their lives. Consider the great egg debate.

> February 11, 2021: *Eating Whole Eggs Bad for Your Heart, Study Shows*[7]
>
> May 24, 2022: *How Eating Eggs Can Boost Heart Health*[8]

Perhaps they should have read an article from 2019 and saved themselves a lot of time. The article's title reads *Nutrition Science is Broken. This New Egg Study Shows Why.*[9]

While the above might cause us to chuckle a bit, it is puzzling that someone can stand before a microphone and repeat the phrase *the science says* to an audience without anyone questioning it. Nobody asks, "How large was the

---

[6] https://www.statnews.com/2023/07/19/marc-tessier-lavigne-stanford-president-resignation/

[7] https://knowridge.com/2021/02/eating-whole-eggs-bad-for-your-heart-study-shows/

[8] https://www.sciencedaily.com/releases/2022/05/220524124839.htm

[9] https://renuebyscience.com/forums/viewtopic.php?t=54

sample for the study?" Or, "Were the result repeatable?" How about the ever-important, "Who did the experimenting, and what presuppositions did they hold going in?" We need to ask these questions because we can all agree with the saying that *if you educate a thief, you only increase his capacity to steal*. Simply because a scientist or researcher makes a statement, that does not mean their statement is a statement of science. Unfortunately, we often conflate scientists making statements with actual scientific statements.

The fact is that science has limitations. Science cannot be an end-all for truth. As an example, if I deliberately overdosed one of my patients on fentanyl, using science, we can learn how that person died. However, science cannot address the morality of my action. Morality is out of the realm of science.

While it can be explained scientifically why the sky appears blue, science cannot address why it is beautiful. Proof of beauty is outside of scientific inquiry because aesthetics are subjective.

While we can understand equations for the effects of gravity and energy, science cannot precisely explain their origin or what they actually are.

Consciousness and logic, which you need to conduct science, cannot be proven through the scientific method. The Universe's origin and all it contains are also out of science's realm because no human observed it coming into existence, and it is not repeatable. Therefore, origins would fall into the realm of history, and many of these topics fall under the realm of metaphysics.

I painstakingly showed you how silly the comment *the science says* is regarding emotional trauma because we are talking about human beings—unique individual persons. While something might prompt trauma in one person, like witnessing a traumatic injury with copious amounts of blood, another might not bat an eye. There is no litmus test for emotional trauma. It is as unique as the people who suffer from it. Blanket statements and snapping fingers don't apply. With that said, let's look at some of the causes.

POTENTIAL CAUSES FOR EMOTIONAL TRAUMA

Certain events or situations can certainly trigger emotional trauma. For example, an individual could be subject to abuse for a prolonged time, like an abusive childhood or years with a violent partner, a hostage situation, or a victim of a kidnapping.

A singular traumatic event can also cause emotional trauma, which can be anything from physical or sexual assault to the death of a loved one or the loss of a home due to a natural disaster or fire. A life-changing traumatic injury accident can also cause emotional trauma.

And then, of course, the culmination of witnessing horrific or high-intensity events, as what First Responders, Law Enforcement, and our military members experience, can also produce symptoms of emotional trauma.

WHO IT AFFECTS

People need practical, shoe-leather answers because emotional trauma can surely impact your nursing staff. Imagine that young CNA who has never witnessed a death or the dying process in someone before, only to stand helplessly by as their beloved resident passes away or learned about the loss after coming back from their days off or vacation. Or even experiencing a resident's traumatic injury fall. Again the Care Center is not the usual place to see a traumatic injury; therefore, it can be traumatic for those not used to seeing that type of painful event.

As mentioned in a previous chapter, emotional trauma can also affect residents who come into your Care Center. Many older residents can feel the frustration of losing their mobility. Some have worked all their lives with the dangling carrot of how wonderful retirement would be, only to have to sell their home and belongings to move into an Assisted Living Facility that will house a minimal amount of what they worked so hard to attain to make their life comfortable. They can feel the frustration of needing help from others. The loss of independence is also a real sting to the ego. Then there are family members who will tell your resident how much they would love to visit, but of course, they are too busy building their own lives.

Aside from the workplace, you can have friends and family members who suffer from emotional trauma, but each can react differently. For example, two individuals can grow up in the same environment, like being subject to a violent alcoholic parent. Because of their upbringing, one could conclude not to have anything to do with alcohol. They realize its negative impact on themselves and those around them and vehemently reject it. Simultaneously, their sibling, who is very close in age and grew up in the same exact environment, will embrace alcohol as a way to cope. What can happen is that the one who rejects the alcohol will sometimes stand in judgment of the one who embraces it because they don't understand that everyone reacts differently to the same trauma. Therefore I would suggest counseling for both.

Perhaps you have or are suffering from emotional trauma. When I speak nationally about this topic, it never goes beyond my notice that some of those sitting before me decided to attend my workshop because they struggle in this area. I will tell you candidly that this is why it breaks my heart when I listen to others address this tough topic. Most, if not all, seem to share the same type of cold erudition I heard in that miserable training I took in 2017.

BE ON THE LOOKOUT

What should you look for regarding emotional trauma in yourself or others? The information I will give you is not exhaustive but is enough to offer you a heads-up and should catch your attention.

Many who suffer from emotional trauma will isolate themselves from others. Depending upon the trauma, they might not want to face other people. Some can suffer from a palpable despondency, a loss of hope for their future, or anything else.

There is also a perceived loss of control for folks in trauma which might cause them to want to control everything around them. You might recognize behaviors like hoarding or obsessive-compulsive disorders among those who feel things are out of their control.

Eating disorders are also highly prevalent among people suffering from emotional trauma and can be expressed in various ways, from overeating to self-starvation and purging. Other types of self-harm are also exhibited in those who suffer, like cutting or pulling out their hair, something I did as a child without much notice by others.

There is also a feeling of being overwhelmed. Folks suffering from emotional trauma may feel unable to concentrate, so even something as simple as ordering off a menu might seem too much to decide. The sad truth is that some might not even remember how they got to the restaurant in the first place! Overwhelming them with more information is not the best thing to do. Individuals who have recently lost a spouse can especially have this feeling. The term *widow's brain* is accurate and describes what these individuals can go through for at least a year after their loss.

There can also be a lack of self-esteem among people suffering from emotional trauma. Depending upon what caused it, an individual might blame themself for the situation that caused their trauma no matter how inappropriate that might be. Or perhaps because they grew up in an environment where everyone around them told them they were worthless or treated them as such, they might buy into that thinking. And while specific words might not come to mind or a particular act someone might have done to them, they are left with an inaccurate impression of themselves that they bought into based upon the negative words or actions imposed upon them.

People who suffer from a singular event might have anniversary reactions on the specific date or season every year that the event occurred. They can suffer from recurrent nightmares where it is hard for them to *turn off* their mind.

Have you ever heard the saying that *hurt people hurt people*? Well, that's possible. One of your residents who carry past trauma might see a *Guy Smiley* in your Care Center and think, *How can you be smiling and happy when I have all this pain inside me?* And because misery loves company, she might consciously or unconsciously do what she can to bring *Mr. Smiley* down to the same miserable emotional level that she is. However, though hurt people can hurt people, many can wind up being the most compassionate because they understand what it's like to be treated shamefully; therefore, they have the desire to lift the burdens of others.

Flashbacks are also prevalent among people with emotional trauma. What's interesting about flashbacks which are a good thing and a sign that the mind is ready to heal, is that they generally happen when the person is removed from the situation and is safe. It is almost as if the mind knows *We're all good, but we got to deal with this. How about now?* So often, when people have flashbacks, they try to stuff that or change their thinking. But the thing to do when a flashback occurs is to consider what triggered that particular memory. When we ponder it, we can then unpack it. The mind and the body will work very hard to address the emotional pain we have experienced as a way to unpack.

Then there is something I refer to as *scrolling the wall*. Since no one knows what audio tapes are anymore, *rolling the tapes* seems a bit archaic. When *scrolling the wall*, just like on social media, you're repeatedly looking back and reliving the situation in your mind. Some people, however, do that with their lives. I know an account of someone who lost a loved one while traveling. Unfortunately, he came home and found them. Every year since his loved one's death, this person would take the same trip to prepare himself emotionally for the moment of walking through the door. It was a ritual that he felt almost guilty about breaking. Then came 2020 when he was forced to break that unhealthy cycle because he could not travel for two years like many of us. The pandemic finally got him out of that yearly cycle of ritualistically traumatizing himself out of some self-imposed guilt he did not need to carry.

THE FEAR FACTOR

What happens when we get into those cycles of *scrolling the wall?* We feel stuck. And the number one thing that keeps us stuck is fear. When I think of fear, I think about the little army men my son used to play with when he was small. While they had everything to advance, those little guys couldn't move forward because of that tiny piece of plastic between their feet. While it allowed them to stand, it did not allow them to advance.

Fear is just like that little piece of plastic between the feet of those little army men. There are a variety of things that can prompt fear. We might be fearful of the future. Perhaps we fear something horrible happening to us, such as what happened to a loved one. It might be a fear of losing resources or other people. The fact about fear is that it constantly lies to us—fear causes us to lie to ourselves about what might happen in the future. We could also lie to ourselves about what happened to us before others because of shame, embarrassment, or false responsibility. Fear never tells the truth!

Of course, since emotional trauma is unique to everyone, you could probably list many more elements. My goal in this chapter was to give you an idea of how impacting emotional trauma can be. In the next chapter, help is on the way.

QUESTIONS FOR THOUGHT

1. Why is the phrase *the science says* not only inaccurate but silly? Why doesn't it work when it comes to emotional trauma?
2. What are some potential causes of emotional trauma? Can you list more?
3. Who can emotional trauma affect? How does it affect your staff?
4. Do you recognize any signs in your staff or residents who might suffer from emotional trauma?
5. What role does fear play in emotional trauma? Can we trust it? Why or why not?

11. Practical Help for the Hurting

When helping anyone, including yourself, with emotional trauma, understand that it is our natural inclination to lean toward what is unhealthy and even destructive when we suffer. When we have thistles up to our chin, our miserable choices to get out of that situation or to help make ourselves more comfortable are startling. Therefore, we must learn to embrace the *opposite* of our natural inclination when experiencing emotional trauma.

TRUTH vs. LIES

For example, we must embrace the truth of our situation to help move forward versus believing lies. Frequently we will think that we will never get better. We will assume that how we feel today is how we will feel for the rest of our lives. And since we can't comprehend living the rest of our lives in that pained condition, some of us strongly desire to take drastic measures.

However, this is not seeing truth. How we feel today is not how we might feel a year from now, six months, or even tomorrow—our emotions ebb and flow. I will never forget when my daughter was about eight years old, and we were playing Monopoly, listening to a radio program. And somehow, something or someone mentioned the word *suicide*. She asked me what that word meant, and I told her. She looked at me and sadly asked why somebody would do that to themselves. I said well, "It's like this Monopoly game. You've got Boardwalk, and I keep landing on it. I'm losing all my money. Suicide would be like quitting the game without realizing that my very next roll of the dice would have resulted in me going straight to Free Parking, where I would pick up that pile of cash sitting there, turning the whole game around after I purchased Park Place!" The truth is that there is hope for us all. While we are still alive, we have the power to change and even use our circumstances to our benefit and the benefit of others, as this author can attest.

Another lie we tell ourselves is, *This event (or series of events) and the emotional trauma that followed is what defines me.* It is the lie that, *This trauma is who I am.* People will define and identify themselves by their trauma. But we are not human doings or human happenings. We are human beings. What happens to us does not define us. Something far greater defines who and what we are, which is found in our inviolable value as human beings.

We can also lie to ourselves, believing, *No one cares about me or what I've gone through.* Or that, *No one will ever understand, no matter how hard I try to explain*. While it might be true that individuals cannot comprehend what we've experienced, they can certainly understand what it's like to feel lonely and suffer from loss, sadness, physical pain, anger, regret, sorrow, or guilt. These feelings are common to all human beings unless you are a sociopath!

We must be patient that while people haven't walked the same exact walk, things they have gone through can prompt the same emotions. Many people have been through similar experiences and are on the other side of their emotional pain. As a result, some might have started an organization to help others facing the same trauma. These might be recovery programs or organizations for individuals who have lost loved ones. I know of organizations that help post-abortive women that are staffed by women who have *been-there-done-that* and whose hearts have healed. People who have been there are people who care and can relate.

One way to help individuals who might believe what is untrue is to show people the truth about themselves. We can let people know they have skills and abilities that are needed in this world. We must remind them that they are loved and that there is a plan and purpose for their life.

We can also ask folks what evidence they have for all their negative self-talk. Part of *scrolling the wall* is internalizing all the negative words and attitudes others imposed upon those who would believe it. But how many of those words are simply lies? So many cruel words have zero evidence to back them up because they're stated by ignorant, envious, or hateful people.

It might also be surprising to learn that the friends and family members who, if we would simply open up and talk to them, are more compassionate and receptive to our pain than we ever imagined. It takes bravery to open up and be vulnerable enough to let others know we need help. If that's you, now is the time to do that.

Why do we hesitate to take that first step? The last lie I'll address here is this thinking that it is a sign of weakness to request help. And when you think about it, I respond when someone in my district calls 9-1-1. Therefore, who do I call? Though I kid a bit, that is sometimes how we think. When we are the ones who help so many others, we don't believe anyone else would be equipped enough to help us. Or when loving folks around us extend their hand, we tend to slap it back because we don't want to be viewed as *helpless*.

If you need assistance, you should ask for it because it's incredible how many other people are in the same boat. You encourage and make an impact on others by admitting that you do need help. How many other individuals who are just as afraid as you are who will then speak up and ask for the support they need, seeing that you have as well?

Also, never rob others of the honor and blessing of helping you during a difficult time. I had a very dear friend who had liver cancer and eventually succumbed to it. He was an individual who was there for everybody at any time, day or night. Suddenly, there he was, a shadow of himself lying on his couch. During one of my visits to him, he said, "Judy, I couldn't believe it. A bunch of guys came here yesterday, and they were mowing the lawn, and they were trimming all the hedges, and they just did a beautiful job cleaning up the yard, and I was too weak to get out there and help them, so I just lay here and wept because I couldn't be out there to help them!"

I replied, "You know what? You have always been there for everybody. Now is the time for everybody to be here for you. Please don't be sad about it. Be thankful and realize this is how they express their great love and appreciation for you. They are now following your example. Please don't ever stop them or feel bad about it. They learned this from you!"

Some people are great counselors. Other people step up as prayer warriors! Others are not so strong in those areas but can mow a lawn, and they can bring a meal or clean a house if you're feeling too overwhelmed to do it. People are standing on the sidelines who would love to show and express their love for you. Let them honor you in that way. Don't slap their hand back from that. And as you see them being there for you uniquely, you can learn how to be there for others if or when that time comes.

EXPRESSING vs. SUPPRESSING

Shortly after my dear friend passed on from liver cancer, his wife happened to have had a doctor's visit. During the appointment, she mentioned that her husband had died. He immediately asked her if she wanted him to prescribe her any depression medication. She looked at him amazed and said, "I'm sad. I'm not sick!" Quite right!

Did something sad happen to you? Are you sad? That's called *normal*. There is nothing to sedate because sadness is a normal human emotion that assigns value to our loss. Because we treat sadness like a mental disorder, our desire is an attempt to suppress normal human emotions with a knee-jerk reaction. It doesn't work!

Our attempts at suppressing, rather than expressing our emotions, only kicks the can down the road because the body and mind want to unpack it, and eventually, we will have to deal with our emotional pain. The pain we feel, especially for a loved one, assigns value to that life. It honors the life of that person! Nothing is worse than having someone who is supposed to be close to you pass away and feel nothing because of how fractured the relationship was. Grief is a gift.

Turning to drugs or alcohol to suppress normal human emotions can lead to more challenges and addiction. You might suggest to your hurting friend, "You need a break. Let's go to the nightclub, have a few drinks, and forget about it all." Unfortunately, while you can *have a few drinks*, you have no idea you could leave that hurting individual off on a terrible path to addiction.

Aside from this, there is also a good reason we chuckle when someone states, "Hold my beer. Watch this!" because alcohol affects the areas of the brain that impact decision-making and impulse control. While what follows in a YouTube clip can be pretty funny, it is not for folks in emotional trauma. Alcohol is a depressant, and depressants don't help people when they're already depressed! Handing someone something that affects their critical thinking skills when they're already having difficulty critically thinking is not the best help. People in emotional trauma need to be as sober-minded as possible because the trauma alone will affect their cognitive abilities. We certainly don't need to offer them liquid courage for the strength to do some pretty regrettable and irreversible actions, making the whole situation far worse than it ever needed to be.

We also have individuals who, to suppress their emotional trauma, will simply refuse to talk about it. They will tell you that nothing is wrong and that everything is fine. However, if pressed, you might get a dramatic, angry response with them blowing up in your face as they yell, "Can't everybody just leave me alone? Why don't people just leave me to myself? I'm fine, I'm fine, for goodness sake!"

Usually, what I do to help folks who *say* they don't want to talk, if the person is sitting down, I will put my hands on my knees and lean over toward them and say, "You know, that was a big reaction to a little question. Maybe it would be best if we took some time and chatted about it. Would breakfast be good tomorrow morning, or would dinner be better that evening?" Remember, *she who talks first loses*! Wait until they give you a time and a day. They need to talk. The fact that they had an explosive reaction because you asked proved it. When I press, sometimes the individual will break down because suddenly they see I won't give up on them like others have who wish to avoid the outbursts at all costs.

Unfortunately, what many people do when someone blows up as they suppress their emotions and refuse to talk is put up their hands and say, "All right, all right, forget I asked anything. I'll never ask you about it again," which is precisely the wrong thing to do. They will be thankful that you were sincere and wanted them to get on the road to unpacking their emotional trauma. The big outbursts are simply a tool to shut down the conversation. Please don't buy it!

ENGAGING vs. ISOLATING

Understandably, pulling back from others might make sense when we are hurting the most. In the short run, selectively isolating ourselves might be reasonable, even healthy and necessary, when our emotional trauma is fresh since more stimulation is not helpful as we attempt to quiet the mind.

However, those who isolate themselves entirely for extended periods will stop going to their usual functions and even quit their job or previous volunteer opportunity that they enjoyed. This isolation can be pretty unhealthy and even dangerous. When we are brokenhearted and left to ourselves, the mind can go to hard places. Unfortunately, others will look around and say, "Has anybody seen Joe? Where is Joe?"

Someone might respond, "I haven't seen him." Then ask yet another person, "Have you seen Joe?"

They might respond, "Nope, I haven't seen him either!"

Unfortunately, knowing nobody has seen Joe, everybody is afraid to pick up the phone and call Joe! We need to check in on people and make sure they're okay. We need to build community again because there are hurting and lonely people among us. Because they pulled back due to trauma, many folks do not know how to re-engage. You can make a significant impact by simply picking up the phone to call, not text, and saying, "Hey, we miss you. There are a lot of people asking about you. How about we go out for coffee or breakfast and catch up? It's been a while. Is Thursday good, or would Saturday be better?"

Whenever someone I know has been through something difficult, I give them a little time until things settle before reaching out. I do this, especially with folks who have an extensive support system of family and friends to allow for a time of adjustment. When I hear that their support system has returned to their usual schedule, I know the hurting individual will have the time to get together. I don't want to take time away from family members or people who might be closer to that person. When they have moved on from the hurting individual to their life priorities, I will usually call to check on the person in emotional trauma and to make plans to get together.

The temptation to pull away from everything and everyone is formidable. Our natural inclination is to isolate ourselves rather than engage with anyone or anything when we are hurting the most. I can personally attest to this powerful inclination.

This pulling back and wanting to curl up into a ball to salve my pain was a strong desire for me in 2011 when I went through an emotionally painful experience that I never imagined I would face. The best way to explain the feeling that came over me at the time was that it felt as if my right arm was ripped from my body. When I recognized that I wanted to pull back and assume the posture of a sow bug, I told my husband that I needed to do *something*. I was either going to do *something*, I had no idea what that would be, or I wanted to quit everything.

My life was already busy, so the luxury of curling up was impossible. I was working on another book, training nationally on other topics, and serving in my fire department while homeschooling my son. Yet, I felt like I needed something new and different that my mind could work on where I could not think of my emotional pain. I needed a fun distraction.

My husband was such a sweetheart through it all. After telling him I felt like I was going to go mad and needed *something*, but I didn't know what, my husband, knowing me very well, looked at me and said, "Well, you love old people. Why don't you get your CNA license and work at the Care Center in town? You can do a little part-time thing. That might help." It was as if a light bulb had gone off! His suggestion was just what I needed.

Going through the class was the perfect therapy. I felt like Mom to those young nursing students. It was so much fun! I noticed that many of them were going through various trials or challenges, and it felt good to be there to offer them encouragement and wisdom. They had no idea I was the patient. I had scheduled an interview a few days before taking my state test. I hadn't interviewed for a job in twenty years. Even so, the DON hired me on the spot! Good thing I passed the examination.

Working in hospice, long-term care, and rehab was physically demanding, but I loved the people I worked with and the residents I held precious. As I mentioned, I was promoted to Assisted Living as a Med Tech. Not one staff member or resident on either the long-term care side or Assisted Living ever knew that for the first year and a half that I worked there, every time I took that forty-five minute drive to work, I was in tears from my broken heart. Once I arrived at the Care Center a few minutes early, I would sit in my car, fix my makeup, walk up to those doors, and then drop that baggage right there. I then proceeded to love, love, love on the residence and the staff. Who at the Care Center knew that I was the patient? Nobody knew. Not one person knew that the one who felt like she needed the most healing was the one who was serving.

Because I dropped that miserable baggage and didn't share it with anyone at the Care Center, you might think I was *suppressing* instead of *engaging* by not talking about it. However, there were appropriate people in my life who knew me well and the situation. Those were the people I leaned on to vent or for council. It seemed that for other folks I wasn't necessarily close to, my heartbreak was all they wanted to discuss whenever they saw me. I needed a break. What helped me a lot was that I could be in a place where I knew it would never be a topic of discussion. The change allowed me to take that needed break and be in a different environment where I could release that baggage at the door and set my focus elsewhere—like on those needing love and care, whether resident or staff.

An amazing thing happens when you're in emotional pain, and you choose to fight the inclination to isolate and instead serve others in physical pain and, thus, for many, emotional distress. When you do the very basic and base for another human being what they cannot do for themselves, that is called *perspective*, which is very powerful. I applied the advice I gave the Administrator, mentioned in a previous chapter, to myself. It worked! The Care Center not only became my *happy place* but where I recognized I could make an impact on other levels.

The truth is, had I not gone through that difficult time in my life though it broke my heart, I would never have worked at that Care Center, I would never have shared this training nationally, and this book would not be in your hands. The most painful event in my life emotionally brought about more good than I could ever imagine.

My heartbreaking situation was delightfully resolved in just a couple of years. Toward the end of 2014, I realized the patient had been cured, and it was time for me to hang up my scrubs. I have a little inspirational book that I read daily in the morning. And on my last day at the Care Center, there happened to be this little poem:

> "When all our hopes are gone,
> 'Tis well our hands must keep toiling on

For others' sake:
For strength to bear is found in duty done;
And (she) is best indeed who learns to make
The joy of others cure (her) own heartache."[10]

Only one change I would make in the above poem. "When all our hopes are *perceived* gone..." But oh, how true those little verses were and still are. Life changing.

LOOK FOR WARNING SIGNS

Have you noticed folks around you who struggle emotionally and are despairing? Could any of these individuals be contemplating a horrific permanent solution? If you recognize reckless or impulsive behaviors out of character for that person, driving recklessly with no care for their safety or that of others, feel free to take that as a warning sign.

Perhaps they are communicating suicidal thoughts. Some individuals will tell you they are suicidal. Let's take what they say seriously. I met with a family who consistently heard a young man share his suicidal thoughts. I chatted with him one-on-one, then met with the family and told them, "You need to take what he's saying very seriously."

They responded, "Oh, Judy, he always says things like that." Not two weeks later, he attempted to take his life. Thankfully, he survived. It was not only a wake-up call for the family but also one for him and a pivotal turnaround in that young man's life.

Please take note of someone who has been depressed and struggling and then has a huge personality change where

---

[10] *Streams in the Desert*, Compiled by Mrs. Charles E. Cowman, Copywright 1925, Cowman Publications Inc., Oct. 30th

they are suddenly upbeat and joyful. They look and feel light and airy when you know nothing significant has changed in their life to cause this positive change in attitude and countenance. Could this possibly mean that they have made a decision? You won't know if you don't ask.

Sometimes we think that if we mention suicide to someone, it will give them the idea. Not true. You're not going to give somebody the idea of suicide who isn't thinking about killing themselves simply because you ask them, "Are you thinking of self-harm?"

They might answer, "No, I'm just going through a difficult time right now. I'm struggling but know I'll figure it out."

However, they might say, "Well, to be honest with you, I can't see any resolution to the situation. I'm tired of feeling this way." Or, "I'm sick of being in this much physical or emotional pain, and I'm done." Do we ever want to leave that person alone? We don't, and we get them help. Many resources are available for the specific challenge for which they might be struggling. If you do your homework, you will find the right match.

WHEN CAREGIVERS STRUGGLE

Anyone who has worked in a Care Facility has experienced the loss of a beloved resident. I don't think it does get easier, but there are ways we can help staff through it. Indeed, it is not the time to debrief on what could have or should have been done better. However, it is the time to bring people together and allow everyone to share their thoughts on the situation and special memories of the individual. Don't pressure everyone to speak. Some people might share something about the individual or their personal feelings and struggles in the situation as others listen on. A few listening might identify with what the more vocal individual shares, and they might think, *Okay, that's what I'm going through too, so all of this is normal.* Therefore they don't feel the need to speak up, but knowing you're providing that forum tells them that you care about them as individuals and that you're serious about any emotional pain they might experience from losing a beloved resident.

Always end the meeting focusing on the positive and the good about the individual. End with an uplifting word. Perhaps you can say something like, "What a privilege it was for all of us to get to serve Mabel in the special way we did. I'm so glad she chose our Care Center. Otherwise, we would never have met her and would never have had the special time with her in her life to care for her in a way that few people can." It also confirms that they have a unique and special place in the lives of those who come through your doors.

Have staff members write uplifting notes for the family. Some individuals did this for my family regarding Clarence. Those notes gave us another insight into Clarence and made us realize how many others loved him as we did. They were very special to us.

QUESTIONS FOR THOUGHT

1. How do you handle death or a traumatic injury with your staff? What has worked for you and perhaps hasn't?
2. What role does fear play in emotional trauma? What is the truth about *fear* that once we realize it, it will no longer have any power?
3. When considering truth vs. lies, what lies do we tell ourselves when suffering from emotional trauma?

4. What are the benefits of expressing rather than suppressing feelings when suffering from emotional trauma?
5. What is your greatest takeaway for engaging rather than isolating when suffering an emotionally tragic event?

12. Grieving and Why We Ask, *"Why?"*

Throughout our final chapter, I think it is essential to tackle the issue of grief. I believe we have some false perceptions about it, which makes grieving harder on the ones who suffer, while those who attempt to help seem no better than Job's unsuccessful comforters.

Also, in this chapter, I will address something that seems to happen instinctively and intuitively yet is not handled or even touched upon by others who speak to the issue of emotional trauma. Therefore, since no one else seems to want to address it or knows how, I will. It doesn't matter who you are; all humans seem to have the same question when faced with the worst day of their life. We ask, "Why?" Over the last pages of this book, I hope to offer an answer as to why we ask, *why*.

OUCH!

I think each of us has had the experience of having a bad sunburn, and someone who didn't realize it gave a friendly, firm pat on the back. They unwittingly slapped our sunburn. That is the best way to describe what it feels like when people who know and care attempt to help us through our emotional pain, yet whose words, in reality, sting. They desire to see us return to *normal* as they offer platitudes that seem trite compared to our loss. The fact is, it's not their fault. Our entire culture appears to fall short when it comes to helping those who grieve.

There seems to be an *app* to consult or a pill for almost everything. *Apps* and prescriptions have become our *go-to* when life goes awry. However, as I mentioned previously, grief is not an *illness*. There is no *app* on your phone or pill you can take to erase it. There is no *cure* because those who grieve are not sick. Neither is there a return to *normal*, new or otherwise. Normal does not exist, with or without trauma and grief, because no matter what, you are not the person you were yesterday. Life is constantly changing; we adjust to our circumstances daily, and there are healthy ways to move forward, whether those life changes are good ones or horrific ones. We don't need folks to inform us that our lives will be different from what it once was. However, they do need to realize we won't be either. Therefore, while sounding kind, the typical blanket responses can feel more like a slap to our sunburn.

The reality is that grief is a life partner. Again, it assigns value to who or what we've lost. It reveals our frailty. It expresses our love. Therefore, emotional suffering is *normal*. Also, all grief is valid. But its intensity and expression are as unique as those suffering from it. Because we don't often realize that grief is normal, life-long, and unique in how we express it, we often wonder why we aren't meeting everyone else's expectations for *getting over it*.

WHAT'S NOT HELPFUL

How do people slap your sunburn rather than help during your profound grief? Several ways will most likely prompt an image in your mind of the one who said something insensitive to you, or you might cringe because you can identify as the sunburn slapper.

For example, when helpful folks share their "me too" accounts, they intend to connect and be relatable. However, the situation suddenly becomes about *them* and *their* loss. While you'd like to see them heal, the last thing you need is someone playing *Can-You-Top-This* with their painful story while you are the one who needs comfort. Perhaps the intent is to show you how much worse things can be or, again, to relate, but few things are worse than someone attempting to transfer their pain or outdo yours while you are already hurting.

Some individuals only want to be viewed as a helper, as if they were doing some great duty. Maybe they are people who love being the ones in the know. They brag to others about how they were *there for you* as they desire to be the go-to person for your pain progress. They might even become upset if you don't fill them in on every detail. However, sincere folks can be corrected in what they should or shouldn't do or say to be truly helpful. You can be candid with folks who are honest about your welfare. You can tell them straight up, "Today, I am just feeling really raw," without them trying to fix or abandon you until you are better so they feel more comfortable in your presence.

You might find that some folks distance themselves from you because of their discomfort with your pain. Much of the slapping of sunburn and people's clumsiness around you is their uneasiness in seeing you hurt emotionally. Perhaps they see themselves in the trauma and don't like it. To protect themselves, folks can become judgemental, blame, or look for excuses. This attitude can foster a host of not-so-helpful or downright cruel statements like:

"Well, he was pretty unhealthy."
"Oh, so she did something dangerous!"
"At least you have other children."

WHAM! And it certainly seems that when you need others the most, they can make you feel most judged by their not-so-helpful comments like:

"Are you *still* crying?"
"Haven't you gotten over *that* yet?"
"You never used to say/do this or that."
"You haven't opened his closet yet?"
"Isn't it time to get rid of this or that of hers?"

For that last one, my response would be, "Who says?" Move the clothes, sell the car, or give things away if and when you're ready. You need affirmation of your grief, not clumsy attempts to erase or *move on* from it. Folks seem to think you aren't doing your grieving right if you don't *get over it* or recover as society believes you should. You need folks to support you in your grief. You don't need clumsy attempts at fixing it or pressing you to return to how you were before the loss or event simply because your suffering makes them feel uncomfortable.

WHAT IS HELPFUL

People can often put their foot in their mouth when attempting to console because platitudes don't work. Why? Because they aren't always accurate. What does work is truth. Be honest with yourself and others. If someone you're not comfortable with presses you for information, it's okay to say, "I don't really feel like talking right now but thank you for your concern,"

Some folks are good with being there for hurting people and will rise to the occasion. It might surprise you who those people might be. They might state, "Though I have suffered a loss, I can't imagine how hard this is for you." Or, "I don't know what to say, but I'd like to be here for you. I can't imagine the pain you're going through, but if it's okay with you, I'd just like to sit quietly with you."

You are alone in your pain because loss and suffering are unique for each individual. Yet, by reaching out to others who have suffered similarly, you have community, which is why you can sometimes feel alone but not lonely.

Surviving and then thriving comes by realizing grief is indeed a life companion. A dear friend of mine, who happens to be a widow, stated it perfectly when she said, "Grief is like a pot sitting on the back burner of a stove. It's just always there. But sometimes, it boils over, and it needs my attention." Her statement is quite accurate—the pot will always be there, but it isn't always boiling over. At the same time, we have full front burner pots with joyful things in them, and that is why people don't understand that we can laugh sometimes, and the next moment we can be in tears. Again, the reason is that grief is a life partner, evidence of the good that was.

Expressing human emotion is good because, after all, you are human! If you're angry, state it. Bottling anger transforms it into bitterness. However, if you are angry, don't let your ire cause you to do or say things you will regret. Step back from toxic people in your life to minimize this risk.

If you're sad, express it. Let the tears flow! As stated earlier, suppressing emotion is a natural inclination but unhealthy. Don't mask it with those who love you and want to help. It's okay to express that you'd rather be with the person who passed on. Wanting to be with your deceased loved one differs from actively seeking ways to join them! However, if this is the case, get help! People love and need you.

SELF-CARE

Self-care is okay and necessary. Don't neglect physical activity, sleep, nutrition, or those beautiful moments that can bring you joy because you feel guilty, allowing yourself opportunities to laugh. Laughter is not inappropriate. It is tremendously healing and helpful. Also, self-care is sometimes expressed as caring for others. You might be the type of person who finds that the best way to care for yourself is by helping others. Only you will know if this applies to you, but if it does, *go for it!*

Protect your thought life. Stop *scrolling the wall* to beat yourself up with the thinking, "What could I have said or done differently?" Protect your thought life by guarding what goes into it. Concentrate on something more elevating and positive when you find your mind in a bad place.

Also, it is easy for our minds to obsess over the future and become fearful. Concerns over what might happen in the future can cause an undue and unhealthy amount of stress. When or if this happens, bring your mind to the current moment and what is true, not what is scary in the future and could be a lie. Be thankful for today. I know it is tough to look through a lens of gratitude when you are grieving. But each day, try to jot down ten things that you are thankful for in your life. They could be anything from the fact that you have hot running water to your daily provision or your loved ones by name. Concentrate on that list, and be grateful.

COMMON THREADS: FIGHT-or-FLIGHT

In answering why we ask, *why* when faced with extreme anguish, I would like to look at what I believe are common threads for getting us to the answer. They might seem unrelated, but they do have something in common. Hang in there with me!

The first of the common threads I wish to address to answer the *why* question for emotional trauma is to consider *fight-or-flight*, which are the body's automatic responses to potentially life-threatening or highly intense situations. If you can relate more to the newly acknowledged *freeze* or *fawn* reactions, please include those as well. However, does that automatic fight-or-flight response still exist?

Not long ago, I tuned into that amazingly technical and scientific channel called *YouTube*. There, I watched a video with a gentleman in a white lab coat with glasses perched precariously upon the tip of his nose, saying that humans no longer have the fight-or-flight response. I was amazed to hear this. He reasoned that we no longer needed this response because we were no longer hunter-gatherers. Therefore, fight-or-flight has evolved out of us. I found his conclusion quite interesting though problematic. Because I will tell you that when I am relaxing and laying on my couch after a long, busy day and my Motorola goes off that we have a *Priority 1* call on the fire department, I will leap off the sofa, jump into my turnouts and then respond to the station or the scene.

Amazingly, this older lady will have all sorts of energy to do compressions, snuff out a fire, or whatever else is necessary. So even though I was exhausted at the end of the day, those stress hormones in my body pushed me off the sofa and helped me do many things during the incident call. Of course, I eventually return to a relaxed state, and I once again collapse on my couch, even more exhausted. That is *fight-or-flight!* It gives me the stress hormone boost I need to flee or fight a fire.

How does fight-or-flight impact emotional trauma? The stress hormones released for the response to *get out of Dodge* when there's danger, or to fight for your life or somebody else's, were only meant for short spurts. People with emotional trauma are constantly at that high level of stress hormones—levels we were never meant to live at continually. High levels of stress hormones wear down the mind and body. And I believe it does give you wrinkles. It's not good, but is fight-or-flight real? Does fight-or-flight still exist in humans? I can attest to it, and I believe you would agree that the answer is, *Yes.* The science guy in the lab coat was wrong. Fight-or-flight remains.

COMMON THREADS: THE CONSCIENCE

The second thread I'd like us to ponder in our quest to understand the *why* question is a consideration of the *conscience*. Same question. Does it exist? Is there such a thing as the *conscience*? Well, we can deny or suppress it, but we will all do one of four things during the Christmas rush if we have been driving around a full parking lot attempting to find a space. If we should see a car that's ready to leave and another has been waiting for that spot, if we pull into it swiftly before that other car that's been waiting, we will all respond in one of four ways:

1. We will *condone* it. "It's not a big deal. It's not illegal!"
2. We will *justify* it. "People have done that to me before. It's about time I did it to somebody else. Woohoo!"
3. We will *deny* it. "That car wasn't waiting for that parking spot. They were waiting for one further down."
4. We will *confess* it. "Perhaps that wasn't a nice thing to do. Maybe I'll just back out and look for a different parking spot."

In that situation and many others, we will either *condone*, *justify*, *deny*, or *confess*. Does this mean that perhaps Jiminy Cricket was right? "Always let your conscience be your guide."

Now, I am not talking about our feelings. Our feelings can fool or deceive us. Our emotions can make us do some pretty foolish and impulsive things! The conscience is different because if you have ever violated your conscience, you immediately sense it. Think of the times that you have violated your conscience. What was the outcome? Was it good? Think about it. If everyone followed their conscience, would we ever have to lock a front door?

If I looked at you and said you have no conscience, would that be a compliment? How do we view people we believe do not have one or have suppressed their conscience? We rightly view them as dangerously broken or fractured human beings.

Therefore if asked if there is such a thing as the conscience, our answer would have to be, *Absolutely!* And oddly enough, it sure seems to be a good thing when we follow it since it is disastrous when we don't.

COMMON THREADS: THE "WHY" QUESTION

I must confess that the *why* question was why I decided to train on emotional trauma and then present it to First Responders, nursing staff, and many others nationwide and include it in this book. When people ask, *Why?* On the worst day of their life, we must ask ourselves, *Can we give them an answer?*

It was after eleven hours (You read that right, the 11th hour!) in that miserable emotional trauma training course I took for my fire department with the woman who prefaced everything with *the science says* that a light seemed to have gone off. Yet another slide, of what felt like hundreds, went up, but this time it had only one word on it. The word was, *WHY?*

Suddenly, it was like an epiphany! Something went off in my mind, and I couldn't contain myself. I quickly sat up in my chair, my eyes wide as I pointed to the slide, saying excitedly,

"Why! Why!" The presenter turned her head swiftly and looked directly at me rather angrily.

The rest of the students in the class also swiftly turned their heads in my direction, looking at me as if to say, "Wow, she's in trouble now!"

I didn't care. I just kept saying, "Why! Why!"

To which the presenter dismissively answered, "Yes, people ask, '*Why*.'"

I said, "No! No! Why do they ask, '*Why*?'"

To which she answered, "The science doesn't know."

Feeling like I wanted to pull my hair out, I asked, "The *science* doesn't know?"

She stated confidently, "No, the science doesn't know."

I said, "Oh. Well, do you know?"

She said, "No, we don't know." And then, *click!* Off she went to the next slide. Not very satisfying.

I cannot fault her because I have seen this repeatedly as I attend lectures on emotional trauma throughout the United States. There is a slide acknowledging that people ask *why* on the worst day of their life, but without any real explanation or how we can answer it, they are off to another slide. When asked why we ask, "*Why*," I watched a prominent psychologist dance around the question and finally respond, "People ask *why* because they're curious. And our response could be that it is none of their business why something bad happened to us." Really? That didn't answer the question. Her answer changed the question! As you know, the *why* question is so much more than our mere curiosity.

When I take a step back and think about some of the horrific and tragic scenes I've witnessed in my nearly twenty years as a First Responder and as the Crisis Care Counselor, when a victim or family member looks at me and asks that guttural *why* question that seems to come from the depths of their soul, do you think they think I have the answer? I've just met them or their person. I may or may not know them. I just stepped into their nightmare. I am the one who needs to get information from *them* about what happened. So do you think it is possible that they actually believe I have the answer to why this horrible thing happens to them?

The remarkable thing about the *why* question is that we understand that some things are okay to say to an individual on the worst day of their life. We realize this because we intuitively recognize something unique about this horrific dynamic. It can cause us to feel that the answer is slightly above our heads. And therefore, it is okay to say something like, "Would you like us to call a Chaplain?"

In fact, corporations and organizations across America realize that they need to acknowledge these particular stresses people face. More and more, I see keynote speakers, including myself, who are invited to address their audience members' emotional and even spiritual needs.

Early on, as I conducted my *LPNequip.org* training for a conference, I decided to check out the keynote address that closed the event. I sat puzzled as the keynote speaker told his audience of about six-hundred people to close their eyes and put their hands on their hearts. As I looked around the room, many had one eye open, looking as if to see if anybody else was doing it. The presenter then began to praise his heart, saying, "Thank you, heart, for beating. Thank you, heart, for keeping me alive. Thank you for being there throughout my life as I need you."

And he went on and on and on and on. And I thought, "*Thank you, heart?*" Yup. Thank you, <u>*heart!*</u>

To express my perplexity with his *heart* exercise, allow me to put it this way. Imagine I made you a cell phone and told you that it would have every *app* you could ever dream of at your fingertips. It even had a beautiful case and all kinds of bling on it. Imagine that I made the cell phone specifically for your purposes, to meet your needs whenever needed. Imagine you take it out of my hands, clutch it to your chest, then mutter as you walk away, "Thank you, *cell phone*, you are so smart. You know just what I need when I need it." Though I wanted to give you more information about the cell phone, I simply shrug and watch you wander away as you continue clutching it to your chest, muttering.

Imagine that after a while of vigorous use, your beloved cell phone acquires a virus. Suddenly you become angry and frustrated because the cell phone you relied on is no longer working for you. A virus is inhibiting you from having and doing what you want. Imagine that you go to this person and that person, asking, "Please, can you fix my cell phone?" As they examine it, they all do the same thing. Completely baffled, they only shrug in exhaustion and hand it back to you.

Suddenly you realize that the one who made it might just have the answer as to why it broke in the first place, and because that individual made it, they can also certainly fix it. Imagine you find me standing exactly where I was when you took it from my hands, and you say to me angrily, "The cell phone you made me isn't working anymore. I really need it. How can you allow it to get a virus? I rely on it. You need to fix this for me right now!"

What if I took that cell phone from your hand and calmly said, "I know you're angry with me and are frustrated with this cell phone. But I want to tell you truthfully that viruses will come and go. Your cell phone will always be subject to viruses. Because of this, here's what I'm going to do, I'm going to leave the virus in your phone, and I'm going to teach you how to navigate despite the virus. In fact, I'm going to teach you how to use the virus to your advantage. I am going to teach you how to do this so well that you will have the ability to help many other people because their cell phones are subject to viruses too." Now, how invaluable would that be? Thus, I propose that the *why* question is a vertical prompt. Allow me to explain.

NATURAL INCLINATIONS

Remember, in the previous chapter, I addressed the fact that our natural inclination is to embrace the opposite of what is actually good for us when we are in a state of emotional trauma. We tend to embrace *lies* versus the *truth*. We *suppress* our emotions, thoughts, and feelings instead of *expressing* them. We tend to *isolate* ourselves from others instead of *engaging*, which is far healthier and has many benefits, like seeing that we aren't alone. Here is another opportunity to embrace the opposite. We need to *pursue* rather than *avoid*.

SHAKING OUR FIST

Many years ago, I met a remarkable World War II Veteran who was very angry. He said, "I went into those Concentration Camps as I liberated those poor people, and with what I saw, there can be no God!"

I said, "Why do you think that?"

He said, "Because if God existed, He would be just, and He would be loving."

Now you might be thinking, *Did she just mention God?* Yes, she did. The mention of God, thankfully, is still not illegal. It is also not illogical. And with over four-thousand world religions, I am not alone in recognizing something or Someone superior to myself. What is tragic is that many are terrified of mentioning God in the equation of emotional trauma. Not because they believe God doesn't exist but because they don't want to be viewed as anti-intellectual if they maintain His existence. And with less than ten percent professing atheism or agnosticism, it makes zero sense that we do not bring God into our discussion on emotional trauma in the United States. We ignore the possibility of God for our topic to our detriment. Hang in there as I continue to answer why we ask, "*Why?*"

My heart immediately went out to that World War II hero. I asked him, "How do you know this God that you're shaking your fist at didn't use you to liberate the people that human beings treated so horribly? How do you know that you aren't the answer to the prayer of those who petitioned God to save them from the horror inflicted upon them by people? How do you know that you were not God's answer?"

Suddenly, his entire countenance changed as if a great weight had lifted off his shoulders. He said, "I'm going to have to seriously consider that aren't I?" We talked a bit further, and he then graciously thanked me.

That gentleman's initial level of anger was very intriguing to me. Because, you see, we are only angry at what exists. We are not angry with what does not. For example, since I don't believe in Cupid, I am not angry with him if there isn't dark chocolate waiting for me on Valentine's Day. Because I know he doesn't exist. However, I will chat with my husband if there is none because he exists and should have left me a proper supply! Again we are only angry with what actually exists. If I sit in my vehicle and try to start my car, I am expressing faith in my experience that my vehicle will start.

When it doesn't, I am angry. My car exists, so my anger is not directed at something I don't believe exists.

The other thing I noticed is that that older man began acknowledging the attributes and character of Someone he said he didn't believe in. How did he know? Because he intuitively, innately realized that God, if He existed, would be benevolent and not malevolent. How is it possible that he already knew the attributes and character of God while at the same time saying he didn't believe in His existence? Because the fact is an anger level and an admission of the attributes and character, along with a pronoun, are all passive intuitive acknowledgments for the existence of God. The Veteran's comments proved he did indeed believe that God existed.

Now, if you are like my *science says* instructor and don't want to take my word for it, read the comments from the following individuals from various scientific disciplines and consider their thoughts on the matter:

2019 Templeton Award Winner,
Theoretical Physicist, Marcelo Gleiser:

> "Science can give answers to certain questions, up to a point. This has been known for a very long time in philosophy, it's called the problem of the first cause: we get stuck.
>
> "Science does not kill God. When you hear very famous scientists making pronouncements like... cosmology has explained the origin of the universe and the whole, and we don't need God anymore. That's complete nonsense, because we have not explained the origin of the universe at all."[11]

---

[11] *Science does not kill God*, Ivan Couronne AFP•March 19, 2019

Sir Fred Hoyle, Astrophysicist & Cosmologist
Plumian Professor of Astronomy and Experimental Philosophy at Cambridge:

"A commonsense interpretation of the facts suggests that a superintellect has monkeyed with the physics, as well as with chemistry and biology, and that there are no blind forces worth speaking about in nature. The numbers one calculates from the facts seem to me so overwhelming as to put this conclusion almost beyond question."[12]

Paul Davies, Physicist, 1995 Templeton Prize Winner, Kelvin Medal from the UK Institute of Physics, And the Michael Faraday Prize:

"There is for me powerful evidence that there is something going on behind it all... it seems as though somebody has fine-tuned nature's numbers to make the universe. The impression of design is overwhelming."[13]

Stephen Hawking,
Theoretical Physicist & Cosmologist:

"The laws of science, as we know them at present, contain many fundamental numbers, like the size of the electric charge of the electron and the ratio of the masses of the proton and the electron... The remarkable fact is that the values of these numbers seem to have been very finely

---

[12] *The Universe: Past and Present Reflections*, Engineering and Science, 11/81, pg. 8-12.

[13] *The Cosmic Blueprint: New Discoveries in Nature's Creative Ability to Order the Universe*, New York & London, Templeton Foundation Press, 1988 pg. 203.

adjusted to make possible the development of life."[14]

Centuries ago, people feared scientific advancements would *threaten* belief in God. In these later supposedly advanced years, people fear that scientific progress will *prove* the existence of God! What an odd turnabout.

And so the answer is, as *fight-or-flight*, prompted by fear, is for our physical survival, the *conscience*, which prompts guilt, is for our moral survival, the *why* question, which is prompted by deep sorrow, is perhaps for our emotional and spiritual survival.

Is it not fascinating that those three painful conditions all humans experience—*fear*, *guilt*, and *sorrow*—are just what you would want to take to a loving Being who perhaps allows them in our lives to pursue Him for their reconciliation?

I must honestly state that it is the complete reconciliation of my own fear, guilt, and sorrow that not only helped me survive years of the effects of my emotional trauma but has allowed me to thrive and help scores of others to do the same.

With over four-thousand spiritual world views, how do so many who speak on this topic not recognize that we are spiritual beings with a hunger for a context in understanding and unpacking our trauma? The answer to the *why* question cannot come from any First Responder, Crisis Care Counselor, Chaplain, emotional trauma instructor, or other human being. It can only be answered by a pursuit of God, Himself. And it is high time to stop denying the truth for

---

[14] *A Brief History of Time—From the Big Bang to Black Holes*, New York: Bantam Books, 1988, pg. 125.

what is intuitive as many die by their own hand due to their deep despair.

WRAPPING IT UP!

Emotional trauma is prevalent across the United States, with folks experiencing great difficulty unpacking it. It does affect each of us, including your staff and residents. I hope you learned to recognize the effects of emotional trauma in others and, perhaps, even within yourself.

My goal was that you would have a greater understanding and if you have suffered from emotional trauma, you will thrive in the midst of it with the hope that one day, you will be a help to others, using your experience as you aid them in making sense of what seems senseless and will realize where to go for, if not an answer, at the very least, a context.

QUESTIONS FOR THOUGHT

1. Why is a return to "normal" impossible with or without emotional trauma?
2. What are some helpful things to say to someone who is grieving?
3. From where did the fight-or-flight response come?
4. What is the source of the conscience?
5. What is the answer to the *why* question? Will you pursue the answer further?

FINAL THOUGHTS

I hope you found this a helpful resource in various ways for your Care Center and valuable for many areas of your life. I am so thankful for the unique opportunities I have had throughout my years on this planet that have enabled me to create such a resource.

I am grateful for all my wonderful mentors who invested their time and talent in me. I owe much to those who continue to provide countless opportunities to wear an array of hats and open doors that enable me to help many others wear theirs with wisdom, grace, and a sense of humor. I trust that passing on what I have learned and observed through the years will save your sanity, time on training glitches and work-related frustrations, and a small fortune in consulting fees.

Though I am thankful for the happy times I have had in my life, I am also grateful for the hard places, which enabled me to learn in ways that an easy life can never teach and thus allowed me to write the final segment in this book.

Feel free to reach out through the *LPNequip.org* website if you would like further training, have questions or comments, or to let us know the impact of this training for you, your Care Center staff, and residents.

In the meantime, enjoy making your Care Center the best home for your residents and home-away-from-home for you and your staff.

With gratitude and admiration,

Judy Salisbury

ABOUT THE AUTHOR

Judy Salisbury has been training and motivating nationally on various topics and in a variety of venues for over thirty years. She is a former radio talk show host and the author of ten books. Volunteering for her local fire department since 2005, Judy serves as a firefighter and the Crisis Care Counselor. For seventeen years, Judy volunteered as an EMT, was also an IV-Tech, and was a certified EMS Evaluator/Trainer.

Drawing from her EMS experience and from her time as a CNA/Med-Tech working in hospice, long-term care, rehab, and Assisted Living, along with a decade of experience as the Power of Attorney for a loved one in a skilled nursing facility, Judy created the training program *LPNequip.org.* A program designed specifically for nursing and leadership staff in Assisted Living and long-term care facilities. Judy shares her unique, lively, informative, and relevant keynote addresses and training from coast to coast.

Judy and her husband, Jeff, are proud parents and grandparents who not only serve together on their local fire department but, in 2023, coauthored the children's book, *Finding Faithful Friends.* Judy and Jeff always enjoy safe, warm, and cozy marshmallow roasts at their home on the outskirts of Mount St. Helens Volcanic National Park in Washington State. For more information and scheduling, please visit *LPNequip.org*.

ANOTHER HELPFUL RESOURCE

"Judy Salisbury, with her powerful and inspired writing, has done it again. Not only is this guide timely, but it has the suggested tools we need to make it through any crisis or calamity. I highly recommend it. Well done!"

JENNIFER SANDS
AUTHOR, SPEAKER, 9/11 WIDOW

www.ingramcontent.com/pod-product-compliance
Lightning Source LLC
Chambersburg PA
CBHW062056270326
41931CB00013B/3103
* 9 7 8 0 9 6 5 7 6 7 8 3 5 *